Sloyd

Or Educational Manual Training with Paper, Cardboard, Wood, and Iron for Primary, Grammar, and High Schools

By Everett Schwartz

Published by Pantianos Classics

ISBN-13: 978-1-78987-174-6

First published in 1893

Contents

Preface..*ix*

Introduction .... *x*

Series One - Paper Work.. 12

Model No. 1. Wall Pocket.. 13

Model No. 2 - Windmill 13

Model No. 3. - Cylinder Wall Pocket 14

Model No. 4. - Cubical Match-Safe 15

Model No. 5. - Oblong Comb-Case... 16

Model No. 6. - Triangular Wall-Pocket 16

Model No. 7. - Square Box 17

Model No. 8. - Square Box 17

Model No 9. - Cone Pin-Holder 18

Model No. 10. - Triangular Pyramid Catch-All 18

Model No. 11. - Square Pyramid Waste-Holder............................... 19

Model No. 12. - Hexagonal Box 20

Model No. 13 - Octagonal Box 20

Model No. 14. - Twelve-Sided Basket.. 21

Series Two - Card-Board Work, Fundamental Forms and Modifications 22

Model No. 1. – Cube 23

Model No. 2. - Square Prism.. 25

Model No. 3. - Triangular Prism 26

No. 4.- Square Pyramid 28

Model No. 5.- Triangular Pyramid.. 29

Model No. 6. - Hexagonal Prism 30

Model No. 7. - Hexagonal Pyramid...31

Model No. 8. - Rhombic Prism..32

Model No. 9. - Octahedron...34

Model No. 10. - Pair of Steps...35

Model No. 11. - Pentagonal Prism...36

Model No. 12. - Pentagonal Pyramid...38

Model No. 13. - Crystal Form...39

Model No. 14. - Octagonal Prism...40

Model No. 15. - Rhombohedron...41

Model No. 16. - Isoscehedron..42

Model No. 17. - Frustrum of Square Pyramid 44

Model No. 18. - Pentagonal Dodecahedron...............................45

Model No. 19. - Greek Cross..46

Model No. 20. - Cylinder..47

Model No. 21. - Cone...49

Series Three - Useful Articles in Cardboard 50

Tools and Material Needed 51

Series Four 68

Model No. 1. - Glove Mender 72

Model No. 2. - Seed Stick...73

Model No. 3. - Round Flower Stick...74

Model No. 4. - Letter Opener 74

Model No. 5. - Square Flower Stick..75

Model No. 6. - File Handle 75

Model No. 7. - Key Label..76

Model No. 8. - String Winder...76

Model No. 9. - Round Ruler 77

Model No. 10. - Paper Knife 77

Model No. 11. – Hone...78

Model No. 12. - Lemon Squeezer. 79

Model No. 13. - Pen Tray 80

Model No. 14. - Cutting Board 81

Model No. 15. - Flower Pot Rest 82

Model No. 16. - A Sugar Scoop 83

Model No. 17. - Clothes Hanger 84

Model No. 18. - Dish Drainer 85

Model No. 19. - Towel Roller 86

Model No. 20. - Sponge Rack 87

Model No. 21. – Blotter 88

Model No. 22. - Nail Box 89

Model No. 23. - Stirring Spoon 90

Model No. 24. - Table Mat 91

Model No. 25. - Coat Hanger 92

Model No. 26. – Ruler 92

Model No. 27. - Bill Holder 93

Model. No. 28. - Book Rack 94

Model No. 29. - Mail Box 96

Model No. 30. - Pulley Block 97

Model No. 31. - Knife Box 98

Model No. 32. - Axe Handle 99

Model No. 33. - Copper Stick 99

Model No. 34. - Set Square 99

Model No. 35. - Photograph Frame 100

Model No. 36. - Try-Square 101

Model No. 37. - Silver Box 102

Model No. 38. - Marking Gauge 103

Model No. 39. - Wall Bracket 104

Model No. 40. - Comb and Brush Case 105

Model No. 41. - Bureau Tray 106

Model No. 42. – Ottoman 107

Model No. 43. - Cabinet 108

Analysis of Models. Series Four 110

Series Five 112

Model No. 1. - Tool Holder 113

Model No. 2. - Gimlet Handle 114

Model No. 3. - Tool Handle 114

Model No. 4. - Bric-A-Brac Stand 115

Model No. 5. - Towel Rack 116

Model No. 6. - Window Box 117

Model No. 7. - Round Ruler 118

Model No. 8. - Drawing Board Rest 119

Model No. 9. - Key-Hanger 120

Model No. 10. - Stocking Mender 120

Model No. 11. Indian Clubs 121

Model No. 12. - Dumb Bells 121

Model No. 13. - Potato Masher 121

Model No. 14. Mallet 122

Model No. 15. - Book Shelves 123

Model No. 16. - Tool Handle 124

Model No. 17. - Tool Handle 124

Model No. 18. - Paper Rack 125

Model No. 19. - Bread Board 126

Model No. 20. - Bill File 127

Model No. 21. - Pulley Block 128

Model No. 22. – Blotter 129

Model No. 23. - Paper Knife 130

Model No. 24. Pen Holder 131

Model No. 25. - Ink Stand 132

Model No. 26. – Easel 133

Model No. 27. - Powder Box..134

Model No. 28. - Napkin Ring..135

Model No. 29. - Butter Stamp..135

Series Six - Forging 136

Model No. 1. - Hammer Exercise...137

Model No. 2. - Bending Exercise...137

Model No. 3. - Round Ring..138

Model No. 4. - Square Ring...139

Model No. 5. - Flat Ring..139

Model No. 7. - S Hook...139

Model No. 6. - Harness Hook..141

Model No. 8. - Staples...141

Model No. 9. - Hook...141

Model No. 10. - Truck Hanger...141

Model No. 11. - Hexagon with Pyramidal Points...142

Model No. 12. - Octagon with Conical Point..142

Model No. 13. - Spindle...143

Model No. 14. - Angle Iron, Parallel Legs..143

Model No. 15. - Angle Iron with Tapered Legs...144

Model No. 16. - V Scarf Weld..145

Model No. 17. - Side Scarf Weld...146

Model No. 18. - Chain Links..146

Model No. 19. - Welded Rings...147

Model No. 20. - Square Rings...147

Model No. 21. - Flat Rings..147

Model No. 22..147

Model No. 23. - Knee Iron...147

Model No. 24. - T Iron...148

Model No. 25. - T Iron...149

Model No. 26. - Clevis...150

Model No. 27. - Hook...151

Model No. 28. - Swivel..151

Model No. 29. 1-2" Suare Headed Bolt..152

Model No. 30. - 1-2" Hexagonal Headed Bolt......................................152

Model No. 31. - 1-2" Square Nut..152

Model No. 32. - 1-2" Hexagonal Nut..152

Model No. 33. - Octagonal Center Punch...153

Model No. 34. - Cape Chisel...154

Model No. 35. - Flat Chisel...154

Model No. 36. - Round-Nosed Lathe Tool...155

Model No. 37. - Cutting-Off Tool..155

Model No. 38. - Side Tool...156

Model No. 39. - Diamond Point...156

Model No. 40. Flat Pein Hammer..157

Model No. 41. - Tongs..157

Model No. 42. - Machinist Hammer..158

Equipment for Forge Shop...158

Preface

The object of this book is to give to teachers a complete system of work, based upon purely educational principles, extending from the kindergarten through the high school; a system that has been tried with success in some of the best schools, and pronounced most excellent by leading educators of the country; a system, too, that the best educated mechanics consider sound and practical as well as progressive. Moreover, it is a system that will set teachers to thinking and inventing for themselves; and, while it will give them an opportunity to learn how to make correctly with tools the models preparatory to teaching, it will cause them to see the vital connection between the Manual Training and the other school work.

Moreover, it is a system that teaches the fundamental principles of of drawing, designing, and construction and also the correct use of all kinds of wood-working and forging tools.

The first exercises in this work are so simple that they can be performed by any child in the lowest primary classes, and are so graded in number, form and drawing as to meet successfully its intellectual growth from day to day.

The book is the outcome of many years experience in teaching and study with the foremost teachers in the United States and Europe; and its chief purpose is to show that Manual Training, in its best forms, can be introduced into the schools of every city, town, and village with success and at comparatively small expense.

The author wishes to acknowledge his indebtedness to Mr. Geo. W. Whittemore, Assistant Master in the Waltham Manual Training School for valuable help in arranging the exercises and models in the forge shop.

Introduction

In the preparation of a system of manual training, the educator should have for his end and aim the educational value of the work. He should also know, and come in such close contact with other school work, that he will see the importance of manual training, and be able, through existing circumstances and conditions, to see and make the connection between it and all other subjects in the school.

The first step, as shown in the kindergarten, must be to train the powers of observation, producing new growth in the mental organism. This is done with exercises of placing, putting, building, - leading up to drawing and construction. These are also forcible means in training the imagination, and inventive skill, and are invaluable lessons in language, number, form and geometry.

There are many kinds of work, founded on or developed from the kindergarten occupations that will serve for the purpose of manual training, with drawing as a component part of each. In drawing, the eye is rendered more accurate, and the hand is brought more completely under the will than by any other exercise; but in itself it is not sufficient, it must be supplemented by its application to work in paper, card-board, wood and other material, and in the making from the drawing that which the drawing represents.

Because paper-work has been used to a great extent in the kindergarten and in the home, it is best, perhaps, to begin with it in the first primary, keeping in mind that the work must form the basis and material for a great many lessons in attention, language, number, form-drawing, reading and writing; and that the article made should be of such a form and nature, and so systematically arranged that there will be a steady growth in all phases of the work.

"But just what shall I do? what can the children make? how can these things be made? what instruments and tools would they need? how can number, language, etc., be taught with it?" These are questions often asked by teachers.

No teacher should feel confined to a certain set of models, but rather, let the desired exercises be embodied in a good model original with the pupil or teacher, being careful to keep the general trend of thought the same. The first series of diagrams will show models and exercises that have been used in Boston schools with success.

For a room of fifty-six pupils the following tools and material would be needed: One thousand sheets of white or colored paper, and about the constituency of good writing paper, cut accurately eight inches square. Obtain this from some wholesale house, sending sample and dimensions; a few ounces of worsted, the colors selected being such that will blend with the colors of the paper; fifty-six hard wood, one foot rulers one and three-eighths inches wide, with beveled edge and graduated into one inch, one-half inch, one-quarter inch, one-eighth inch spaces; fifty-six lead pencils ("Dixon's American Graphite, M," is good), with fine point; fifty-six rubber erasers; fifty-six pairs good pencil dividers. that can be easily adjusted; fifty-six pairs good six inch scissors; fifty-six darning needles. All these, excepting the paper, can be kept in a neatly made cloth case, with an apartment for each tool and kind of material, and can be rolled up or hung on the inside of a closet-door.

Series One - Paper Work

Example No. 1. - Have the children sit squarely in their seats, both feet on the floor. Have them hold up their right hands, left hands, the index finger of right and left hands. Have them touch with an index finger the front edge of their desks, which is the edge next to them; the same exercise with the back, right, and left edges, the back right corner, the back left, front right, and front left. Begin here by having the children, one at a time, give directions.

Example No. 2. - Choose as many pupils as there are rows of seats, selecting those who need the training the most, and have them help in giving out the work. Have a certain place for every thing and teach their name and uses as they are given out, and let it be done in the following manner: Hold up a ruler before the pupils, write the word on the board, and have them speak the word, then will the ruler, the written and oral word be associated in the mind.

The work should be given out in the following order: Place the paper on the desks so that one of its edges will be parallel with and about two inches from the front edge of the desk and directly in front of you. Now repeat with the paper Example No. 1.

Example No. 3. - Take up the rulers, find the long mark near Fig. 1.

Question. - How far is it from there to the nearest corner?

Answer. -One inch. (Repeat this with two inches, three inches, and four inches.) Have them see that the corner of the ruler most used is where the one inch begins. Place the corner of the ruler on the back left corner of the paper and have the edge of the ruler parallel with the back edge of the paper; then place a fine point .on the paper directly below the four inch mark, with the pencil held in a vertical position.

Question. - How far is the point from the back left corner?

Answer. - Four inches.

Question. - How far is it from the back right corner?

Answer. - Four inches.

Question. - What have you done to the edge?

Answer. - Bisected it, or divided it into two equal parts.

Question. - What shall we call the point?

Answer. - The middle point, or point of bisection.

The pupils now bisect the other edges of their paper

Example No. 4. - Teach now opposite edges, opposite corners and points. Place the ruler so

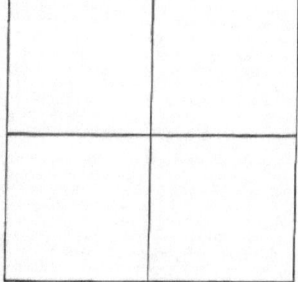

that the edge shall connect the point in the back edge with the point in the front edge. To hold the ruler firmly, divide it into thirds with the thumb and the fore and middle finger. Hold the pencil as you are taught to hold the pen, then join with a line the points connected by the ruler, beginning at the back; join the remaining opposite points, beginning at the left in drawing the line.

Model No. 1. Wall Pocket

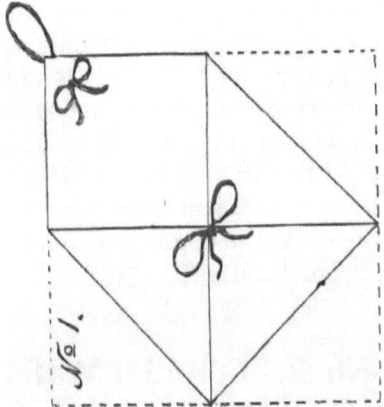

Example No. 5. - Now put the model, which is a wall-pocket, where all can see it, and without direction have them fold their papers as the folding is done in the model. Have the worsted cut to the right length and teach them how to thread it into the needle, and to catch up the corners and make a loop to hang it by, as shown in the diagram, and model No. 1 is finished.

Model No. 2 - Windmill

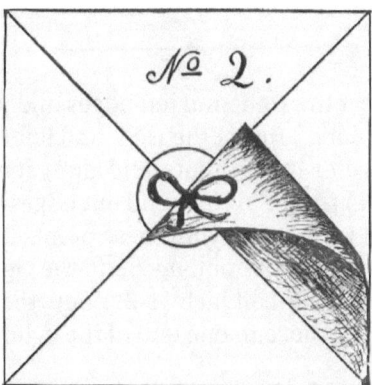

Place the paper in position.

Exercise No. 7. - Place the ruler from back right to front left corners, and draw the diagonal. Draw the other diagonal.

(Teach here that the square is now divided into four equal parts, and the middle point is found).

Exercise No. 8. - Take up the dividers, loosen the adjusting screw and open them so that the distance between the pivot and marking points will equal one inch. Place the pivot point at the centre of the square, grasp the dividers at their extreme upper end, with the tips of the thumb and fore-finger, and then make a circle by twirling the dividers, keeping the hand and arm in one position.

Teach here, the circle, centre, circumference, radius, and diameter.

Exercise No. 9. - Take up the paper with the left hand, and with the scissors, beginning at the corners, cut along the diagonals to the circumference of the circle. Bend the upper corner of the right quarter, the right corner of the front quarter, the lower corner of the left quarter, and the left corner of the back quarter to the centre. Catch up these corners as indicated in the diagram, sewing through the back. The pupils should fold and sew the form from the model and not from dictation).

Model No. 3. - Cylinder Wall Pocket

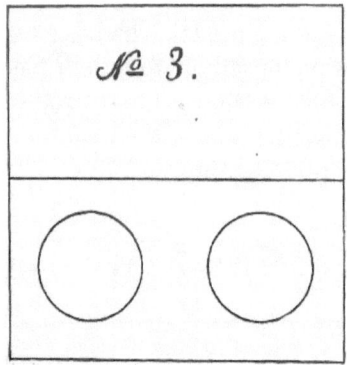

Show the model. Bisect the right and left edges and join these points with a line. (Teach here the oblong.) Bisect the right and left edges of the front oblong, connect with the ruler these points, and along its edge in the oblong, place points one inch (1) from the right and left edges. Open the dividers one and one-fourth inches (1 1-4") and with these points as centers inscribe circles. Cut out the circles and upper oblong. Bend the right edge of the oblong over the left edge lapping one-half inch (1-2"). Sew these together forming a cylinder. Sew one circular piece to one end of the cylinder and use the other for a hanger.

Model No. 4. - Cubical Match-Safe

№ 4.	1			
3	2	4		
	5			
	6			

Bisect all edges of the paper.

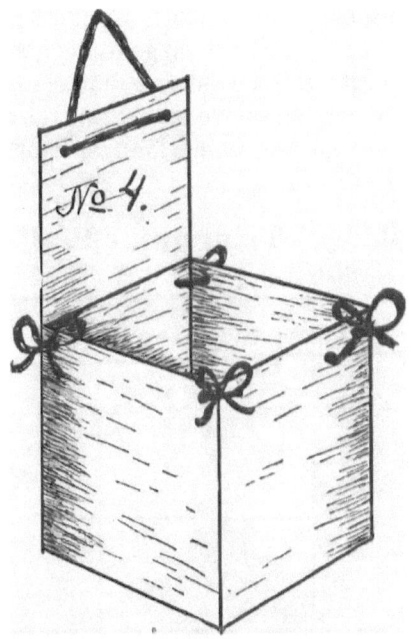

Exercise No. 10. - Bisect all halves of edges.
(Teach here quadrisecting and opposite points).
Join with lines all opposite points.
(Teach from the model, the number and shape of the faces and the shape it takes when unfolded). The square to the right of the back left square is No. 1, the one in front of 1 is 2, the one to the left of 2 is 3, the one to the right of 2 is 4, the one in front of 2 is 5 and the one in front of 5 is 6. Cut, fold, and sew from the model.

15

Model No. 5. - Oblong Comb-Case

№ 5.	*1*	
3	2	4
	5	
	6	

Have the pupils examine the model, teach the oblong, its faces, etc., and its relation to the cube. Let a number of them go to the board and draw the shape as it would appear if unfolded. Be sure that all can see the construction, and then, without directions, have them draw the diagram. Cut, fold, and sew the oblong, excepting one face with a loop for hanging as in the cube.

Model No. 6. - Triangular Wall-Pocket

№ 6.	*1*	
3	2	4
	5	

Present the model. Teach here the triangular prism, and have the pupils, by measuring, see that the sides of the triangular ends are equal.

Exercise No. 11. - Draw on the board a square, construct within the square on one of its sides an equilateral triangle, by means of arcs with a pair of chalk dividers; and following the plan as with the oblong, have the pupils draw their diagram. Fold and sew the triangular prism, leaving one oblong face with loop for hanging.

Model No. 7. - Square Box

Present model. Have pupils obtain measurements from the model, draw diagram, cut away the corners, fold and sew without dictation.

Model No. 8. - Square Box

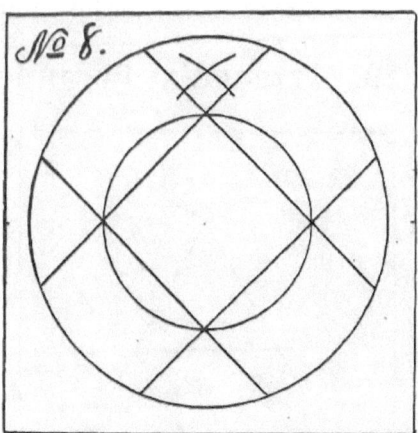

Bisect right and left edges and find center of square. Open the dividers 3 1-2' and with the center of the square as a center inscribe a circle. With the same point as a center inscribe a 4" circle. Place the ruler from right to left across the paper through the center and where it crosses the circumference of the smaller circle, place points.

Exercise No. 12. - With these points as centers and with a radius equal to 1 3-4' describe arcs above the center, between the circumference of the circles. Place the ruler across the paper through intersection of arcs and the center, and where it crosses the circumference of the smaller circle place points. Join all adjacent points and extend the lines to the circumference of the larger circle. Cut along the circumference of larger circle, cut away triangular corners, fold up the sides and sew from the model.

Model No 9. - Cone Pin-Holder

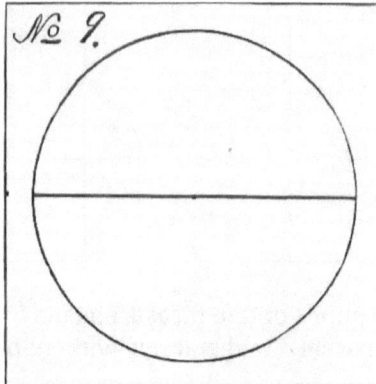

Find center of square, open dividers 3 1-2 , from the center inscribe a circle and draw a diameter to the circle from right to left, using points. Unfold the model and have them cut, fold and sew, leaving loop at the base for hanging.

Model No. 10. - Triangular Pyramid Catch-All

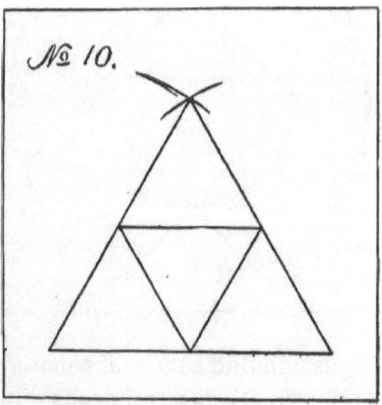

(Present model and then unfold, to show that all sides and the large triangle of which they are composed are equilateral triangles.) On the left edge of

18

the square and 1' from the front left corner, place a point; place a point opposite on the right edge. Join with the ruler these points, and beginning 1" from the left point, draw a line 6" long in the square. Construct on the hoard on a given line, by means of arcs, an equilateral triangle. (Have the pupils see the construction of the triangles in the folding and then draw their diagrams). Bisect all edges of the large triangle, join all adjacent points, fold and sew, leaving one side with loop for hanging.

Model No. 11. - Square Pyramid Waste-Holder

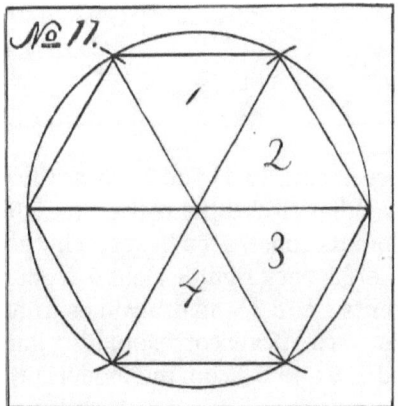

From the center of the square inscribe a 7" circle. Draw a right and left diameter to the circle. Open the dividers equal to the radius of the circle.

Exercise No. 13. - Place the dividers at the right end of diameter and with arcs cut the circumference above and below. Draw corresponding arcs from left end of diameter, dividing the circumference into six equal parts. Join all adjacent points, making a hexagon within the circle. Join all opposite points, dividing the hexagon into six equilateral triangles. The back triangle is No. 1, back right No. 2, front right No. 3, front No. 4, front left No. 5, and back left No. 6. Unfold the model and have the pupils see the construction. Cut, fold, and sew, leaving loop for hanging.

Model No. 12. - Hexagonal Box

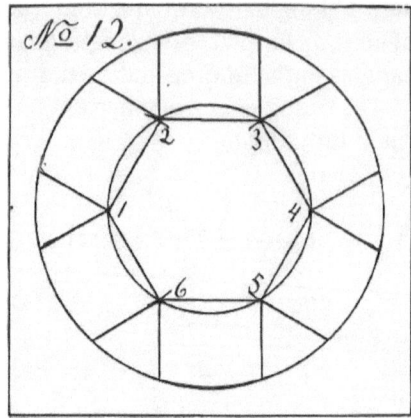

From center of square inscribe a 4" and 7" circle. By placing points in the right and left sides of smaller circle, divide the circumference into two equal parts, and from these points construct a hexagon in the circle. Number the left corner 1, the back left 2, back right 3, right 4, front right 5 and front left 6. Join, with the ruler, points 1 and 3, and draw lines from these points to the circumference of larger circle. Draw corresponding lines from points 2 and 4, 3 and 5, 4 and (3, 5 and 1, 6 and 2. From the model cut, fold, and sew.

Model No. 13 - Octagonal Box

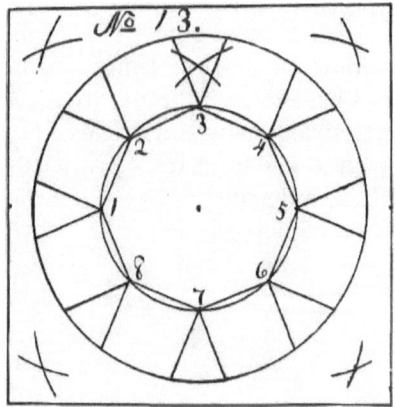

Exercise No. 14. - From center of square inscribe a 4" and 7" circle. Divide the circumference of smaller circle into two equal parts, with points in the right and left sides. Open the dividers 1 3-4" and from these points make intersection of arcs above the center and between the circumferences of cir-

20

cles, join with the ruler intersection of arcs with center and where the ruler crosses the circumference of smaller circle, place points, dividing it now into four equal parts. From the right point with radius equal to 1 3-4" describe ares in the back right and front right corners of square, repeat the exercise from the remaining points, making intersection of arcs in all corners of square. Join with the ruler opposite intersections, placing points in circumference of smaller circle, dividing the circle now into eight equal parts. Join all adjacent points, making an octagon. Join with the ruler, points 1 and 4, and from these points draw lines to the circumference of larger circle, from points 2 and 5, 3 and 6, 4 and 7, 5 and 8, 6 and 1, 7 and 2, 8 and 3. draw corresponding lines. From the model cut, fold, and sew.

Model No. 14. - Twelve-Sided Basket

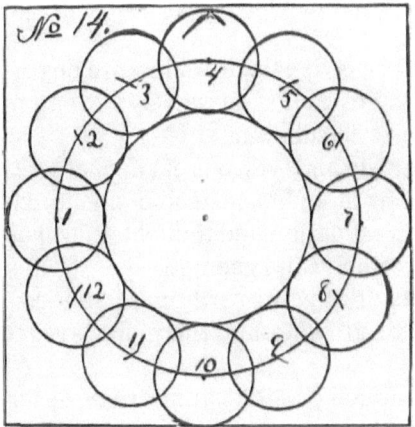

From center of square inscribe a 4" and 6" circle, indicate ends of horizontal and vertical diameters by points as in the octagon. Open the dividers equal to the radius of larger circle and from the right point draw arcs across the circumference above and below, draw corresponding arcs from remaining points, dividing the circumference into twelve equal parts. With these twelve points as centers and a radius equal to 1" inscribe circles. Cut around the outer edge of figure, and cut out the elliptical figures inside. Sew, so as to make flaring sides.

Series Two - Card-Board Work, Fundamental Forms and Modifications

Tools and material needed. - A drawing board; some rulers, pencils, erasers, shears and dividers, as were used in the paper series; as many sharp-pointed shoe knives as there are pupils: one-half dozen ten cent cans of Le Page's Liquid Glue; one thousand sheets of white paper, the same as in other series, cut twelve inches by seventeen inches; one thousand sheets of white card-board, of good quality and a little thicker than a postal card, cut twelve by fourteen inches. Send to some wholesale house for samples, and have the cutting done by them.

The object of this work is to help, in an intense degree, in teaching the many subjects that have to do in a direct way with number and form, and forms the basis of future calculations.

This is taught intuitively and with a great deal of interest, as the pupils think and work out their thoughts. Instead of memorizing rules that others have made through investigation and thought, they make their own rules, compile their own arithmetic and geometry.

The models being made of white card-board, renders them very valuable as a series of models for drawing, and therefore saves the cost of a set made of plaster or wood.

The pupils can invent many modifications of these forms, and no matter how far advanced a class may be in number and form work, these models will always be found useful material.

Such as the following can be given in square and cubic measure: Make a box to contain nine cubic inches. Make a box of different shape to contain the same number of cubic inches.

This is also valuable work for the teaching of concise and correct English, and the pupils become acquainted with the use of terms that are best learned in connection with real work.

The work is done with thicker and tougher material than was used in the paper series, and one sees that, in order to do the work, it requires all the skill of hand and mind formerly acquired, and a systematic growth in both.

To test the real growth of ideas and skill of hand, free hand drawing should be taught in connection with it, and also have them draw the same diagrams of the card-board forms on paper, free hand, then cut and fold.

As the models are arranged in the series one can trace the growth of one form from another, but in some cases forms that should come early in the series are put in later, on account of the difficulties in making; but in such cases they can be made of paper in their true position, and afterwards in card-board.

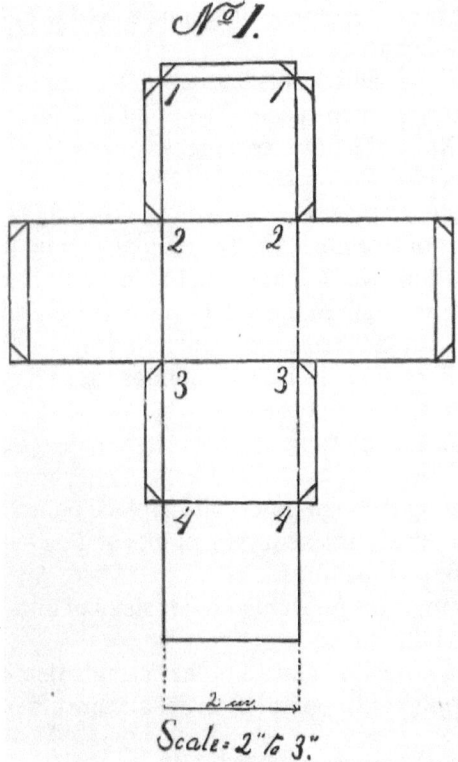

Model No. 1. – Cube

Present a cube to the class, and develop the idea of its form when unfolded, as with the cube in the paper series.

This series of models being entirely closed on all sides, it is necessary that there shall be laps or margins, adhering to the sides for gluing. Have the pupils tell how many laps are needed, and where. When this is clear in the minds of the pupils, erase what may have been drawn on the blackboard as an illustration. and, for a lesson in attention and accuracy, have them draw the diagram from dictation as follows, being careful to give directions slowly, concisely, and not to repeat them if possible:

Bisect the back edge of the paper; place the corner of the ruler at this point, so that the short edge of the ruler will coincide with the back edge of the paper; along the edge of the ruler, place a point four inches below the point of bisection. Place points directly opposite on the right and left edges of paper. Connect the three points with ruler, having the six inch mark rest upon the middle point. This middle point shall be the middle point of a two inch line. Draw the line. Place the corner of ruler at the right end of this line so that the short edge of ruler shall exactly coincide with the line, and, beginning at the right end of line, let fall a perpendicular along the edge of ruler, eight and one-fourth inches in length.

Beginning at the upper end of this line set off a one-fourth inch space, and below this point four two inch spaces. The point one-fourth below the horizontal line is point No. 1, the point two inches below No. 1 is point No. 2; below No. 2 is No. 3: below No. 3 is No. 4.

From the lower end of this line draw a perpendicular two inches to the left; connect the left ends of two horizontal lines, placing and numbering points as before. Connect points No. 1. extending the line one-fourth of an inch to the right and one-fourth inch to the left. Connect points No. 2, extending the line two and one-fourth inches to right and left; draw a corresponding line through points No. 3; connect right ends of lines extending through Nos. 2 and 3; connect the left ends of these lines.

Connect points No. 4, extending the line one-fourth of an inch to right and left.

On the line extending through points No. 2, place points a one-fourth of an inch from each end: place corresponding points on line extending through No. 3, and connect opposite points.

Construct similar margins on right and left sides of upper square; and on the square below the middle square.

On the upper horizontal line place a point one-fourth of an inch from the right end. Join this point with point No. 1; cut all corners of all margins in like manner.

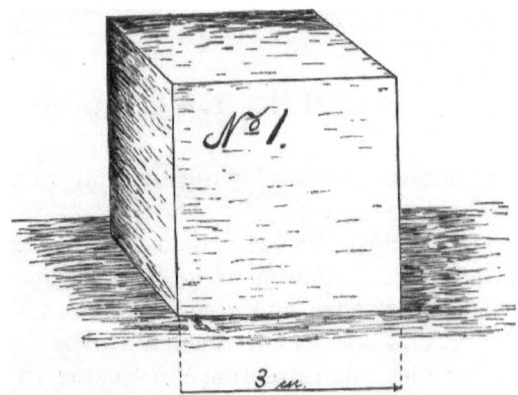

Transfer the drawing upon card-board to a scale of two inches to three inches, or the making of a three inch cube.

Have the class tell along which lines to crease for folding. This should be done along the edge of the ruler with the point of a sharp knife, drawing the knife toward you in a cutting position and cutting the card-board half way through.

Now with the shears cut along the outer edges of the whole diagram. Then cut away corners of margins. Fold so that the creases shall be on the outside and the margins inside.

Spread a thin coating of glue upon the outside of margins, and glue carefully together, one side at a time.

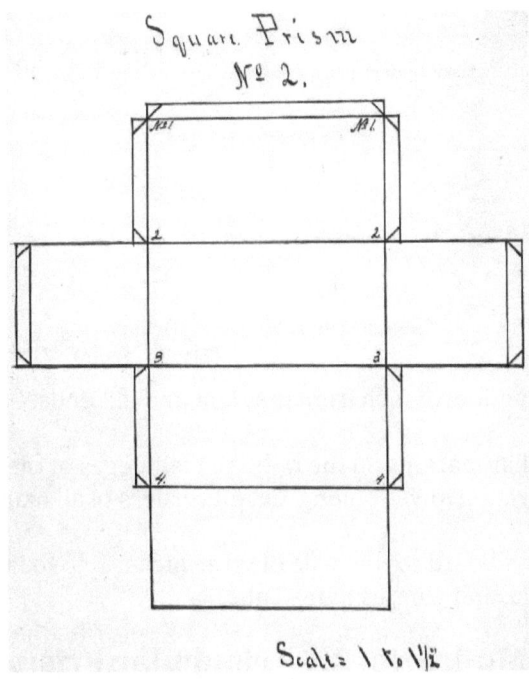

Square Prism
№ 2.

Scale: 1 to 1½

Model No. 2. - Square Prism

Bisect the back edge of paper.

Place a point on the left edge four inches from the back left corner. Place a point directly opposite on the right edge.

Place a point midway between points.

The point last placed shall be the middle point of a four inch horizontal line. Draw the line. From the right end of this line let fall an eight and one-fourth inch perpendicular. From the lower end of this line draw a horizontal line four inches to the left. Connect the left ends of horizontal lines.

In the right vertical beginning at the upper end set off a one-fourth inch space and below it four two-inch spaces. Place corresponding points on left vertical. The points on verticals one-fourth inch from the upper ends are points No. 1; those two inches below are No. 2; those two inches below No. 2 are o. 3, and so on down.

Join points No. 1, extending the line one-fourth inch to the right and left. Join points No. 2, extending the line two and one-fourth inches to the right

25

and left. Draw a corresponding line through points No. 3, then connect points No. 4, extending the line one-fourth inch to the right and left.

Connect the right and left ends of the lines extending through points No. 2 and No. 3. On lines drawn through points 2 and 3.

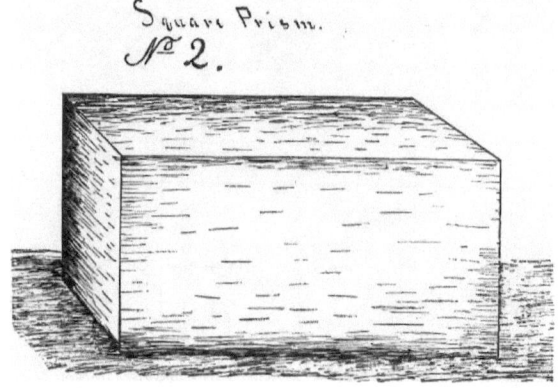

Place points one-fourth inch from the right and left ends. Connect opposite points.

Construct similar margins on the right and left edges of the upper oblong, and the one above the lower oblong. Cut all corners of all margins as in the cube.

Transfer on cardboard to the scale of three inches to two inches.

Crease, cut, fold, and glue, as in the cube.

Model No. 3. - Triangular Prism

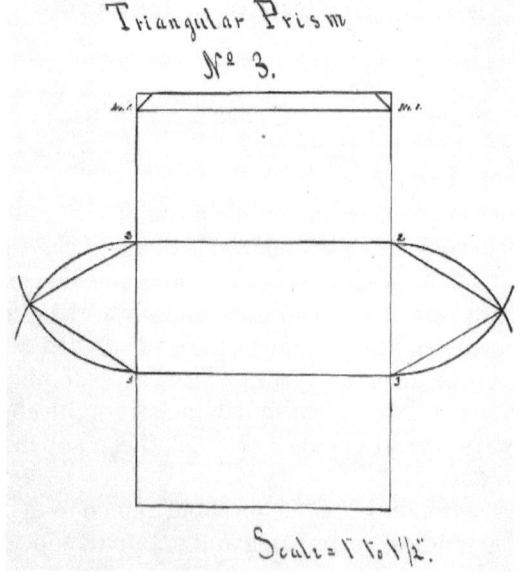

With chalk dividers construct upon the black-board an equiangular triangle, upon a given line, by means of arcs.

Directions for drawing diagram:

Bisect the back edge of the paper. On the left edge place a point four inches from the back left corner; place one directly opposite on the right edge; also place one midway between points. The point last placed shall be the middle point of a four-inch horizontal line. Draw the line. From the right end of this line let fall a perpendicular six and one-fourth inches in length. From the lower end of this line draw a perpendicular four inches to the left. Connect the left ends of horizontal lines.

On these vertical lines place points one-fourth inch from their upper ends and below set off three two-inch spaces, numbering points as in the cube and square prism.

Join all opposite points. Cut the corners of the upper margin as in the cube. Open the dividers equal to the length of the short side of the oblong; place the metal point at point No. 3 to the right; place the pencil point at point No. 2; beginning there, construct an arc about two and one-half inches in length to the right.

Triangular Prism

№ 3.

Place the metal point at point No. 2; construct an arc to the right, intersecting the preceding arc; join intersection of arcs with points 2 and 3.

Construct a corresponding triangle on the left side of the same oblong.

Transfer to card-board to the scale of two inches to three inches.

Crease, cut, fold, and glue, using the circular margins on the sides of the triangles.

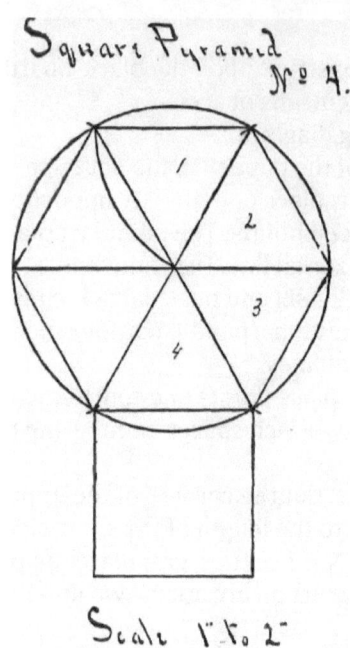

Square Pyramid
№ 4.

Scale 1". to. 2"

No. 4.- Square Pyramid

Place the paper so that the long edges will be parallel with the front edge of the desk. Bisect the back edge of the paper; four inches from this point, directly towards the front edge, place a point; with this point as the center, construct a four-inch circle; draw a horizontal diameter of the circle; from the ends of this diameter construct a hexagon within the circle; connect all opposite points in hexagon.

Square Pyramid
№ 4.

The upper triangle will be side No. 1; upper right triangle, No. 2; lower right triangle, No. 3; and lower triangle No. 4.

With the upper right corner of upper triangle as a center, construct a circular margin on left side of triangle No. 1.

28

The base of the lower triangle shall be the upper side of a square; construct the square.

After transferring drawing to card-board, to a scale of one to two, cut out, preserving the circular margins on triangles Nos. 1, 2, and 3; crease, fold and glue.

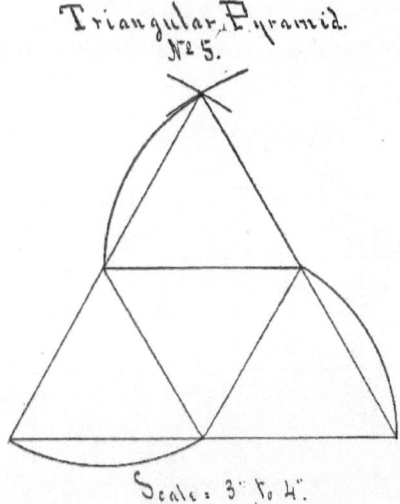

Triangular Pyramid.
№ 5.

Scale: 3" to 4".

Model No. 5.- Triangular Pyramid

Place paper so that the long edges will be parallel with the front edge of desk. Bisect the front edge of paper.: three inches from this point and directly towards the back edge of paper place a point; with this point as a center, draw a six inch horizontal line; using this line as a base, construct a six inch equiangular triangle by means of arcs; bisect all sides of this triangle, join points of bisection in right side with point in left side; connect both of these points with center of base.

Triangular Pyramid.
№ 5.

Open the dividers equal to the length of side of small triangle; place the metal point at lower right corner of upper triangle; with this point as a center construct a circular margin on left side of upper triangle; construct similar margins on the base of lower left triangle, and on the right side of lower right triangle.

Transfer drawing on card-board to a scale of three to four; cut, crease, fold and glue.

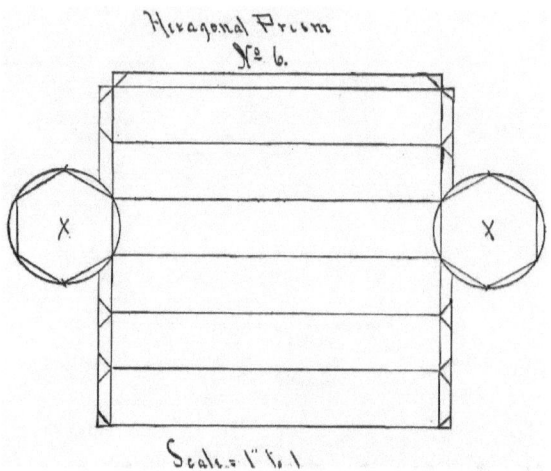

Model No. 6. - Hexagonal Prism

Place paper so that the long edges of paper will be parallel with the front edge of desk; bisect the back edge of paper; two inches from this point and directly in front, place a point; with this point as a center draw a six inch horizontal line; this line shall be the upper edge of an oblong six by six and one-fourth inches; draw the oblong; on the right and left sides of oblong, beginning at the upper edge, set off a one-fourth inch space, and below it six one inch spaces; join all opposite points.

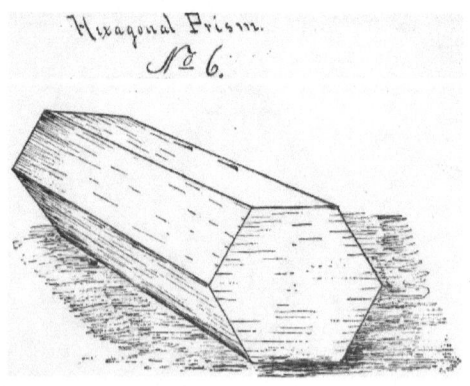

30

Open the dividers one inch, and with the lower and upper right corners of fourth oblong; as centers construct an intersection of arcs to the right.

With an inch radius and intersection of arcs as a center, construct a circle; from the lower and upper right corners of this oblong construct a hexagon within the circle; in the same manner construct a hexagon on the left side of this oblong.

Construct one-fourth inch margins on right and left sides of all oblongs, except the one on which the hexagons are constructed, cutting corners as in cube.

Transferring drawing to cardboard to a scale of one to one, cut, crease, fold, and glue.

Model No. 7. - Hexagonal Pyramid

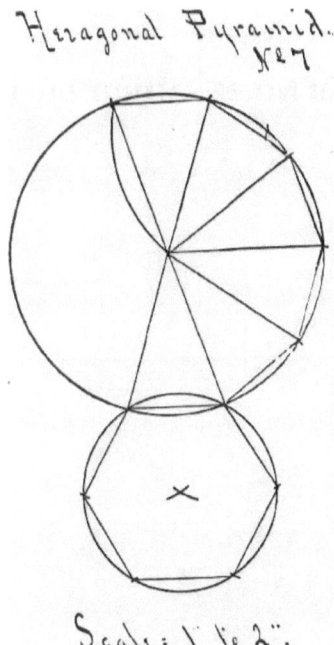

Hexagonal Pyramid.
No 7

Scale: 1" to 2".

Place paper so that the long edges of paper will be parallel with the front edge of desk; bisect the back edge; four inches directly in front of this point, place a point; with this point as a center construct a four-inch circle.

Beginning at lower side of circle, and having dividers open a distance of one and one-fourth inches, lay off six spaces in the circumference of the circle, working upward to the right; join all points in the circumference with the center; draw all chords to arcs, except the greater arc; construct a circular margin on left side of upper left triangle.

31

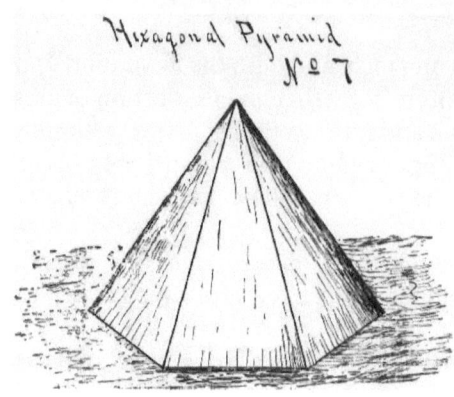

The base of the lower triangle shall be the upper side of a hexagon drawn within a circle; construct the hexagon.

Transfer to card-board to a scale of one to two; cut, crease, fold and glue, using circular margins on hexagon.

Model No. 8. - Rhombic Prism

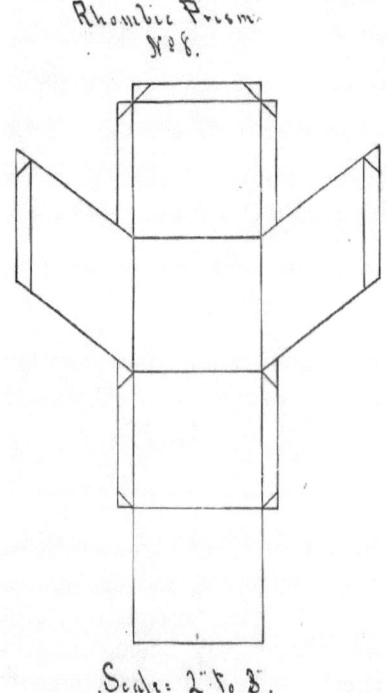

Place paper so that the short edges of paper are parallel with the front of desk; bisect the back edge of paper; place a point two inches directly in front of this point; with this point as a center, draw a two inch horizontal line: this line shall be the back edge of an oblong two inches by eight and one-fourth inches: construct the oblong.

On the right and left edges of oblong, beginning at upper edge, set a one-fourth inch space, below it four two inch spaces; join all opposite points.

The point one-fourth of an inch below the upper edge is No. 1, and so on.

Place points on the lines one-half inch above points three and four; join with the ruler point two in the left with the point one-half inch above three in the right; draw diagonally upward to the left from point 2 a line two and one-fourth inches in length.

Join with the ruler point 3, to the left, with the point one-half inch above the point 4, to the right; draw a line diagonally upward from point 3, to the left, two and one-fourth inches in length; connect the left ends of these lines. On these lines one-fourth of an inch from left ends place points; join opposite points; from corresponding points draw a similar figure on the right side of same square.

Rhombic Prism.

No 8

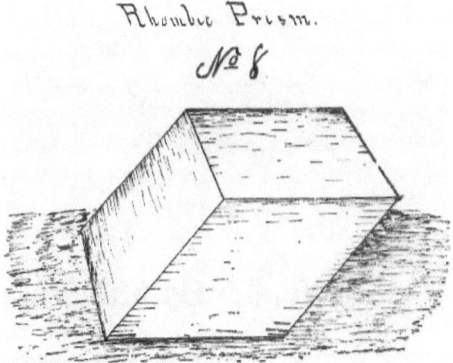

On right and left sides of upper square and the one above lower square, construct one-fourth inch margins, cutting all corners as in cube.

Transfer to card-board to a scale of two to three.

Cut, crease, fold and glue.

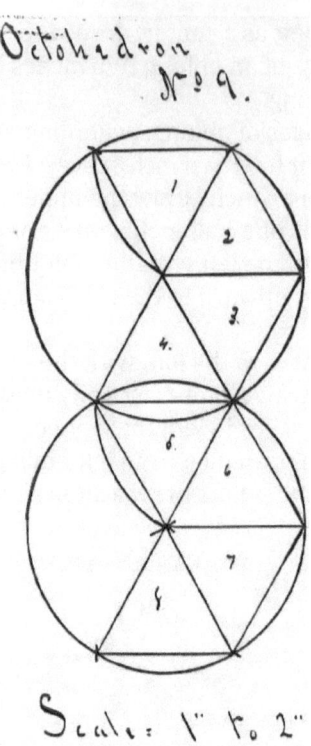

Scale: 1" to 2"

Model No. 9. - Octahedron

Place paper so that the long edges shall be parallel with the front edge of desk; bisect the back edge of paper; four inches directly in front place a point; with this point as a center draw a three inch circle.

Place the ruler in position to draw the horizontal diameter - where the ruler crosses the circumference place points; using these points, divide the circumference into six equal parts; connect all these points with the center.

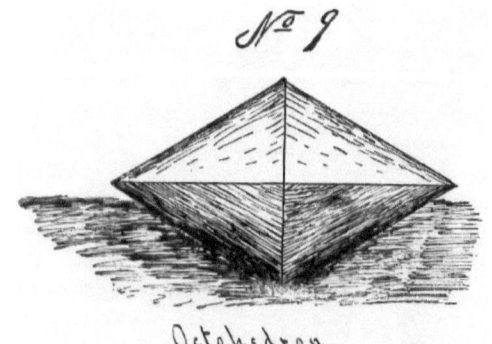

Nº 9

Octohedron.

34

Draw chords of all arcs except the greater. On the left side of upper triangle construct a circular margin, on the base of lower triangle construct an equilateral triangle by means of arcs; with the intersection of arcs as a center construct a three-inch circle and within the circle, triangles as above with circular margin on upper triangle.

In the first circle the upper triangle is No. 1; the upper right, No. 2; lower right, No. 3; and lower triangle No. 4. In the second circle, the upper triangle is No. 5; the upper right, No. 6; lower right, No. 7; and lower, No. 8.

Transfer to a scale of one to two; cut, crease, fold and glue.

Model No. 10. - Pair of Steps

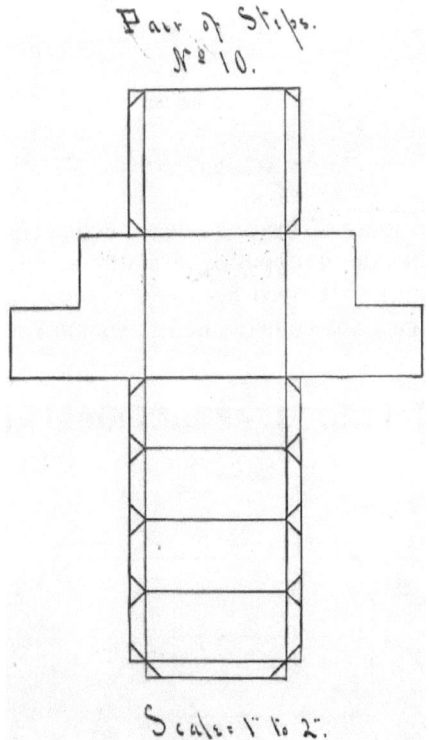

Pair of Steps.
Nº 10.

Scale: 1" to 2".

Place paper so that the short edges will be parallel with the front of desk; bisect the back edge; four inches directly in front of this point place a point; with this as a center draw a two-inch horizontal line, which shall be the upper edge of an oblong two by eight and one-fourth inches; draw the oblong.

On right and left sides of oblong, beginning at the upper edge, set off a one-fourth inch space, below it two two-inch spaces, below these four one-inch spaces; join all opposite points.

Continue the upper side of second square one inch to right and one inch to left; continue the lower side of the same square two inches to right and two inches to left; from the right end of last line draw a one inch vertical line; from the upper end of this line draw a perpendicular to the line one inch to the left; from the left end of this line draw a one inch vertical line.

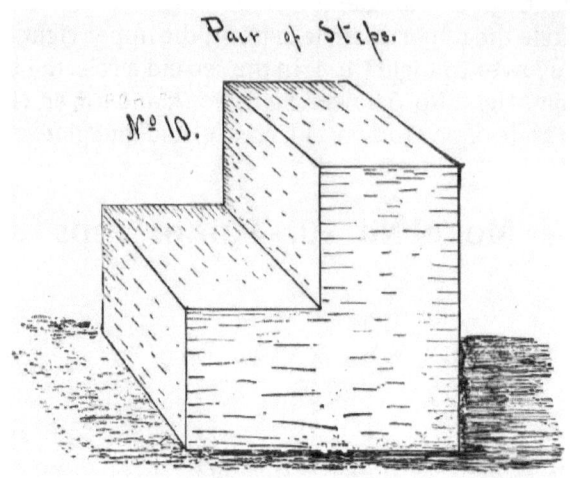

Construct a similar figure on the left side of second square.

On the right and left sides of upper square and the four oblongs, construct one-fourth inch margins, cutting corners as in cube.

Transfer on cardboard to a scale of one to two; cut, crease, fold and glue.

Model No. 11. - Pentagonal Prism

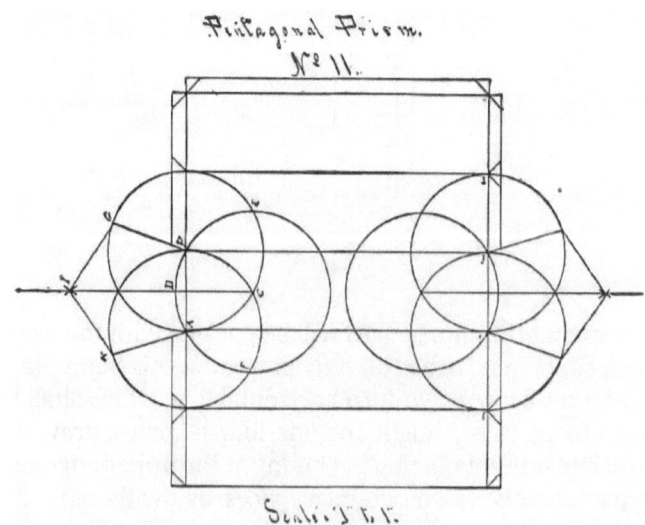

Place the paper so that the long edges will be parallel with the front of desk; bisect the back edge, two inches from this point and directly towards the front edge, place a point; this point shall be the center of a six inch horizontal line; draw the line; this line shall be the upper edge of an oblong six inches by seven and three-fourths: draw the oblong.

On the right and left sides of oblong, beginning at the upper edge, set off a one-fourth inch space and below it five one and one-half inch spaces; join all opposite points.

Mark the lower left corner of oblong No. 3, A; and the upper left corner B; with A and B as centers draw two three inch circles; mark the intersection of these circles at the right, C; join this point with intersection of circles to the left and extend the line indefinitely to the left; with C as a center draw a three inch circle; mark where this circle crosses the line that joins the intesection, D; mark where the circle intersects the upper circle in the upper right, E; and where it crosses the lower circle in the lower right, F; connect with ruler points E and D, and mark where the ruler crosses the lower circle in the lower left H; join with the ruler points F and D and mark where the ruler crosses the upper circle in the upper left G.

With a radius equal to one and one-half inches and with G and H as centers, draw intersection of arcs to the left on the line passing through points C and D.

Mark this intersection I; join B and G; G and I; I and H; and H and A, forming a pentagon.

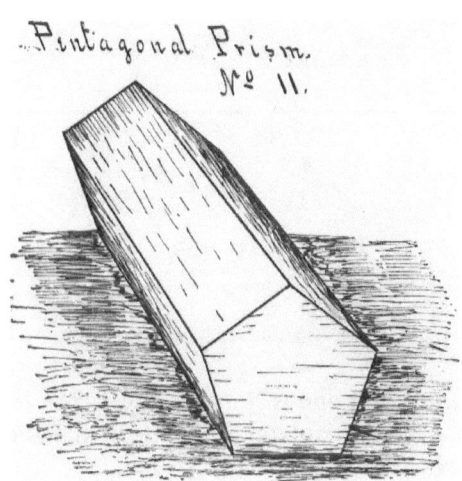

Pentagonal Prism.
Nº 11.

Draw a similar pentagon on the right side of same oblong; on the right and left sides of all oblongs, except No. 3, construct one-fourth inch margins, cutting corners as in cube.

Transfer drawing to card-board to a scale of one to one.

Cut, crease, fold and glue.

Model No. 12. - Pentagonal Pyramid

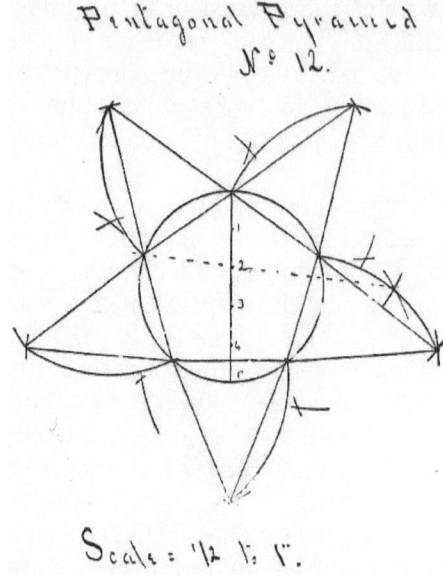

Place paper so that the long edges shall be parallel with the front of desk; find the center of paper; with this point as a center, draw a two- and one-half-inch circle; draw its vertical diameter and divide it into five equal parts.

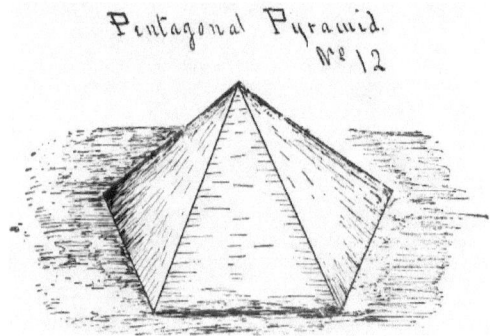

The point below the upper end is No. 1.: below it, No. 2; and so on.

With a radius equal to the diameter and ends of diameter as centers, draw an intersection of arcs to the right.

Place the ruler across the circle through point 2 and intersection of arcs; where the ruler crosses the circle to the left, place a point. A line drawn from this point to the upper end of diameter is one side of a pentagon: with the dividers set off the remaining sides. Each side shall be the base of an isosceles triangle having a slant height of two inches, with its apex pointing outward.

Construct circular margins on alternate sides of all triangles.

Transfer to a scale of one-half to one; cut, crease, fold and glue.

Model No. 13. - Crystal Form

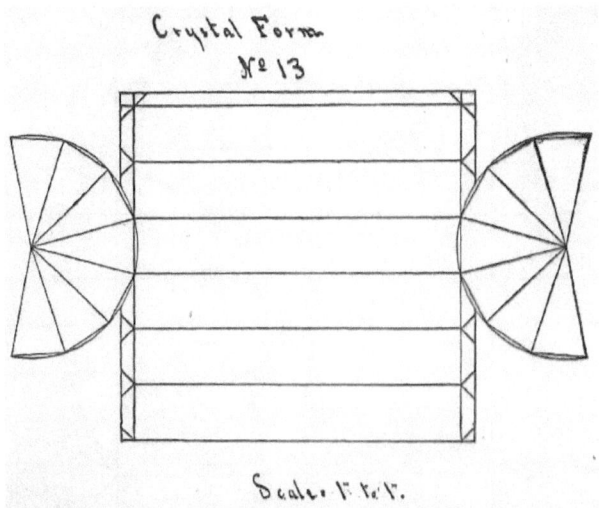

Place the paper so that the short edges shall be parallel with the front of desk; bisect the back edge; four inches in front of this point place a point; this shall be the center of a six-inch horizontal line; draw the line: this line shall be the upper edge of an oblong six inches by six and one-fourth inches; draw the oblong. On the right and left sides of oblong, beginning at the upper edge, set off a one-fourth inch space and below it, six one-inch spaces; join all opposite points. The right side of the third oblong shall be the base of an isosceles triangle having a slant height of two inches and the apex pointing outward. With this apex as a center, and a radius equal to the slant height of triangle, draw a circle.

Draw within the circle five triangles equal to the one already drawn, draw three above and two below.

On the left side of same oblong draw a similar figure; on the right and left sides of all oblongs, except the third, construct a one-fourth inch margin, cutting the corners as in cube.

Transfer to a scale of one inch to one inch, cut, crease, fold and glue.

Model No. 14. - Octagonal Prism

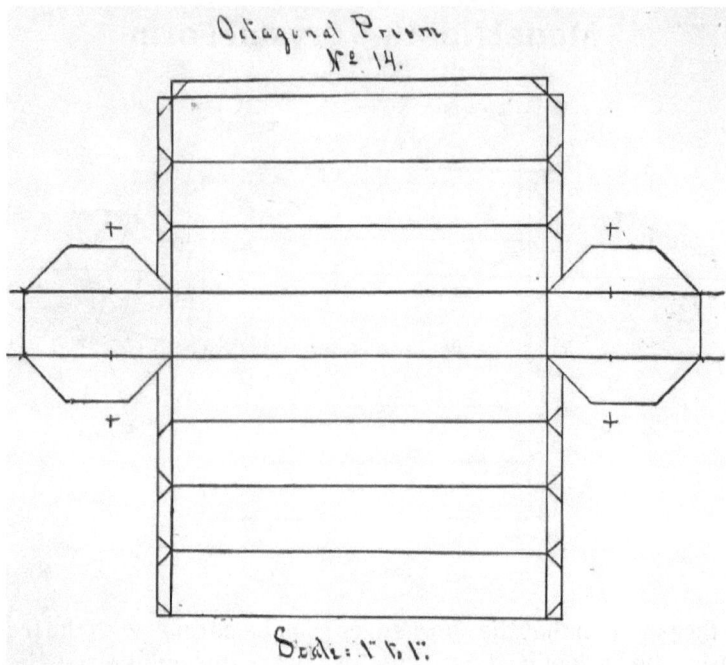

Place paper so that the long edges will be parallel with the front of desk; bisect the back edge; place a point directly in front of it; with this point as a center draw a six-inch horizontal line.

This line shall be the upper edge of an oblong six by eight and one-fourth inches; construct the oblong; on the right and left edges, beginning at upper edge, set off a one-fourth inch space; below it, eight one-inch spaces; join all opposite points.

Continue upper and lower edges of fourth oblong indefinitely to right and left; open the dividers one inch and with the lower and upper right corners of fourth oblong as centers, draw arcs intersecting the extended lines to the right; with these intersections as centers and a one-inch radius, draw arcs above and below.

With the upper right corner of oblong No. 3 and the lower right of No. 5 as centers, and same radius, draw arcs intersecting arcs last drawn; connect with ruler the upper right corner of oblong No. 4 and upper intersection of arcs and from the upper right corner of oblong No. 4 draw a line diagonally upward to the right, one inch long; from the upper end of this line draw a one inch line, directly to the right; with the right end of this line as a center and a one inch radius, draw an arc intersecting the extended lines diagonally downward to the right. In the same manner complete the lower and right sides of octagon.

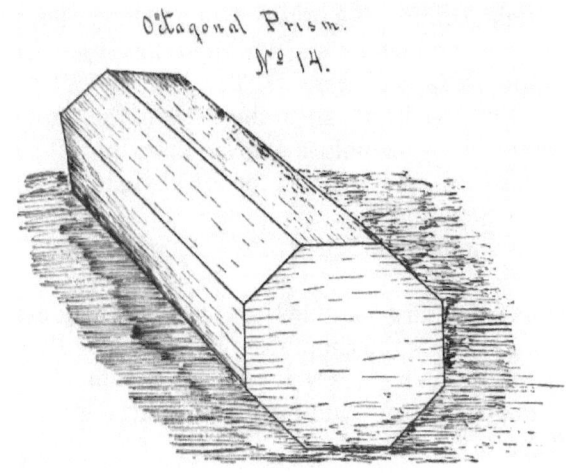

Octagonal Prism.
Nº 14.

On the left side of oblong No. 4 construct a similar octagon; on the right and left sides of all oblongs, except No. 4, construct one-fourth inch margins, cutting corners as in cube.

Transfer to a scale of one to one; cut, crease, fold and glue.

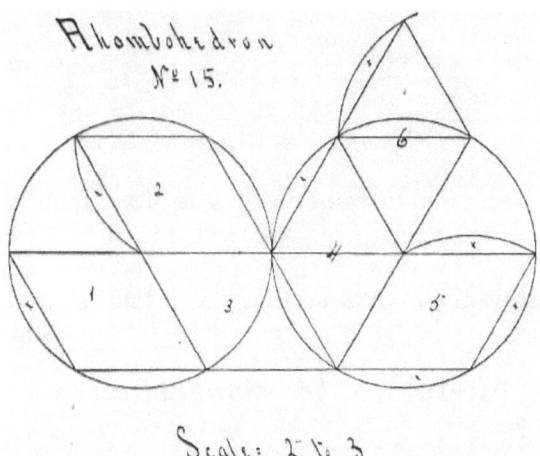

Rhombohedron
Nº 15.

Scale: 1 to 3

Model No. 15. - Rhombohedron

Place paper so that the long edges shall be parallel with the front of desk; bisect the left edge; bisect the right edge; connect points of bisection; on this line four inches from the left end place a point; four inches to the right of it place another; with these points as centers, draw two four inch circles; from ends of diameters divide the circumferences into six equal parts.

In circle to left, connect upper left point with lower right; the left, with lower left; lower left with lower right; upper left with upper right; and upper right with right.

41

In circle to the right, connect the upper right and lower left points; the lower left and lower right; lower right, and right; lower left and left; left and upper left; and upper left and center.

On the upper side of upper triangle in the circle to the right construct an equiangular triangle with apex pointing upward; on the left side of this triangle construct a circular margin; connect the lower right point in circle to left with lower left in circle to right.

On the left side of upper rhombus in the circle to left construct a circular margin.

The left rhombus in left circle is side No. 1; the upper rhombus, No. 2; the one to right of No. 1 is No. 3; the rhombus including upper left and lower left triangles in the circle to the right is No. 4; the lower right rhombus in same circle, No. 5; and the rhombus including the upper triangle and one constructed upon it, No. 6.

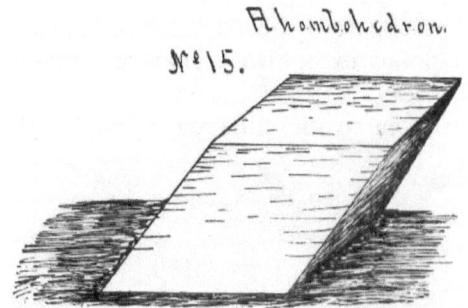

Rhombohedron.

Nº 15.

There should be circular margins on left side of No. 1; on left of No. 2; on upper left of No. 4; on upper, lower, and right sides of No. 5; and upper left side of No. 6.

Transfer to a scale of two to three. Cut, crease, fold and glue.

Model No. 16. - Isoscehedron

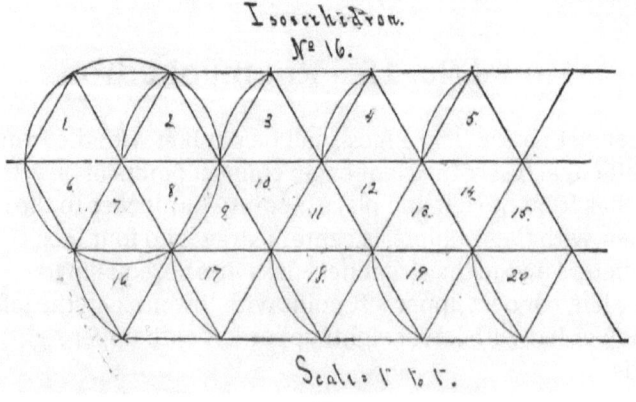

Isoscehedron.

Nº 16.

Scale 1 to 1.

42

Place paper so that the short edges will be parallel with the front of desk; bisect the right and left sides; join opposite points; three inches from the left end of this line place a point. This shall be the center of a four inch circle; draw the circle; from the ends of diameters construct a hexagon within the circle; continue the outer edges of the upper and lower triangles indefinitely to the right; on the lower edge of the lower triangle construct an equilateral triangle, its apex pointing downward; from the apex of. this triangle draw a line parallel With the extended line above.

From the upper right corner of upper triangle set off on the upper line four two inch spaces; from the apex of lower triangle set oft' on lower line four two inch spaces; join all opposite points with lines that shall be parallel with upper right and upper left sides of hexagon.

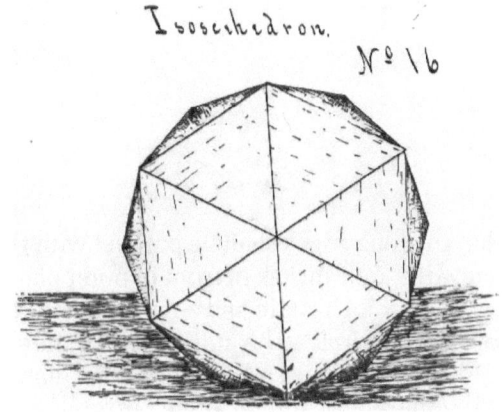

The five upper triangles pointing upward, beginning at the left, shall be numbered 1, 2, 3, 4, and 5; the ten triangles in the middle, 6, 7, 8, 9, 10, 11, 12, 13, 14 and 15; the five triangles below pointing downward, 16, 17, 18, 19 and 20.

There should be circular margins on the left sides of the upper five and the lower five triangles and on the left side of No. 6. Transfer the drawing to cardboard to a scale of one to one.

Cut, fold, crease and glue.

Model No. 17. - Frustrum of Square Pyramid

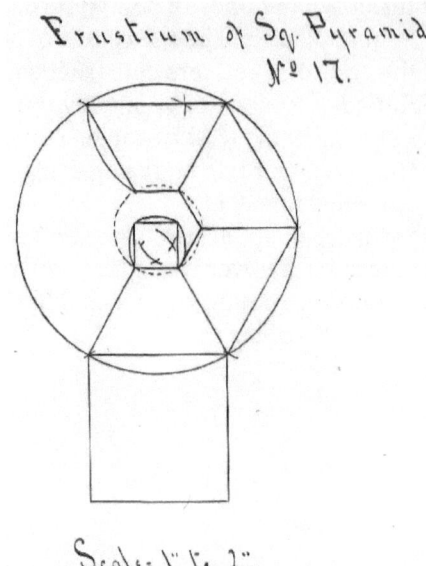

Place paper so that the long edges shall be parallel with the front of the desk; bisect the back edge; four inches in front of point place a point J with this as a center, draw a four inch circle and a one and one-fourth inch circle, the one and one-fourth inch circle to be indicated by a dotted line; place points in circumferences indicating ends of horizontal diameters; from these points divide the circumferences into six equal parts.

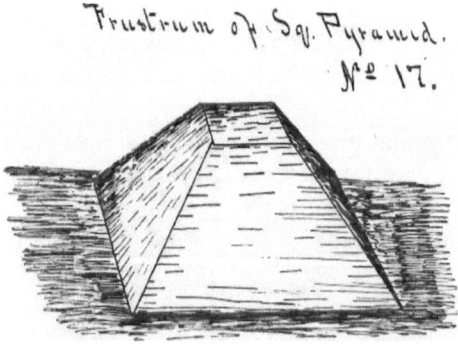

In both circles connect the upper right points with upper left; the upper right and right: the right and lower right; and the lower right and lower left.

Join the upper left corners; the upper right; right; lower right; and lower left. On the upper side of lower frustrum erect a five-eighths square; on the upper, right, and left sides of this square construct circular margins.

Construct a circular margin on left side of upper frustrum.

The base of upper frustrum shall be the upper edge of a square; construct the square.

Transfer to a scale of one to two, and cut, crease, fold and glue.

Model No. 18. - Pentagonal Dodecahedron

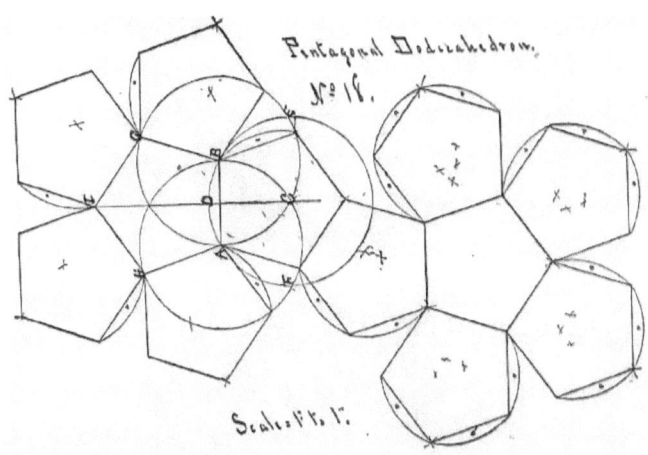

Place paper so that the short edges will be parallel with the front of desk; bisect the back edge; six inches from this point, directly towards the front, place a point; this shall be the center of a one and one-half inch horizontal line; draw the line, marking the left end A, and the right end B; on line A B construct a pentagon as in pentagonal prism.

The upper right corner is C, the upper left, D, and the upper, E. Join with ruler C and D. and draw a line one and one-half inches long to the left from D; join with the ruler C and A and draw a line one and one-half inches long- diagonally downward to the left from A. With the outer ends of these lines as centers, and a one and one-half inch radius, draw an intersection of arcs to the left; join points making a pentagon; on all remaining sides of first pentagon construct a similar pentagon.

On the lower left side of lower pentagon construct a pentagon; on the lower side of this pentagon construct a pentagon; on remaining sides of last pentagon construct pentagons.

On the series of six pentagons above there shall be circular margins on the left side of upper right; on the lower left side of upper left; on the lower right side of lower left; on the upper right side of lower; on the upper side of right.

On the series of six below, there shall be circular margins on the upper left and lower left sides of the upper pentagon; on the upper left, left, and lower left sides of left; on the left, lower, and right sides of the lower left; on the lower, lower right, and upper right sides of the lower right pentagon; and on the lower right, upper right, and upper left of the right pentagon.

Transfer drawing to a scale of one inch to one inch; cut, crease, fold and glue.

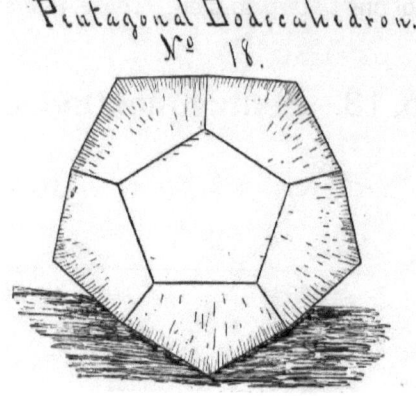

Pentagonal Dodecahedron.
Nº 18.

Model No. 19. - Greek Cross

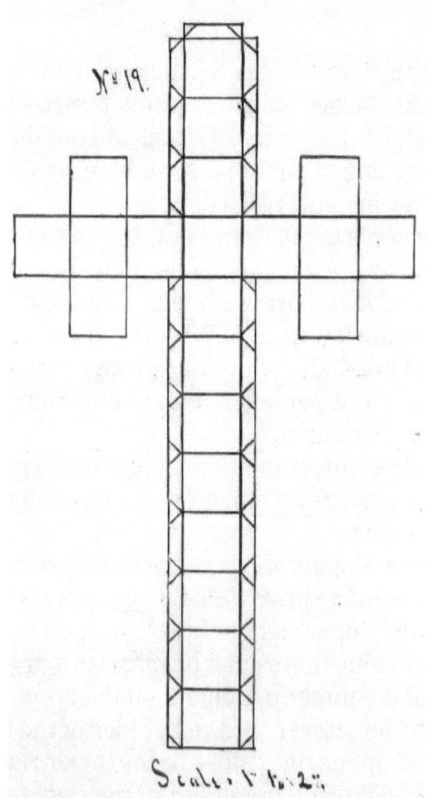

Greek Cross.

Nº 19.

Scale 1" to 2".

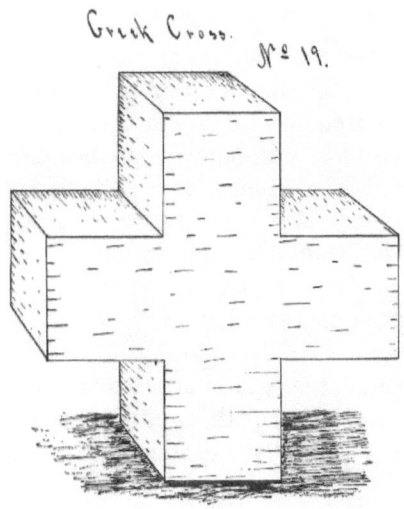

Greek Cross. N° 19.

Place paper so that the short edges will be parallel with the front of desk; bisect the back edge; two inches directly in front place a point which shall be the center of a one-inch horizontal line; draw the line. This line shall be the upper edge of an oblong one inch by twelve and one-fourth; draw the oblong; on the right and left sides of oblong, beginning at upper edge, set off a one-fourth inch space; below it twelve one inch spaces; join all opposite points.

Extend the upper and lower sides of fourth square three inches to the right and three inches to the left; connect the right and left ends of these lines; on these lines place points one inch and two inches from their right and left ends; connect opposite points, extending lines one inch above and one inch below; connect the upper and lower ends of these lines.

On the right and left sides of series of twelve squares, except the fourth square, construct one-fourth inch margins, cutting corners as in cube.

Transfer to a scale of one to two, cut, crease, fold and glue.

Model No. 20. - Cylinder

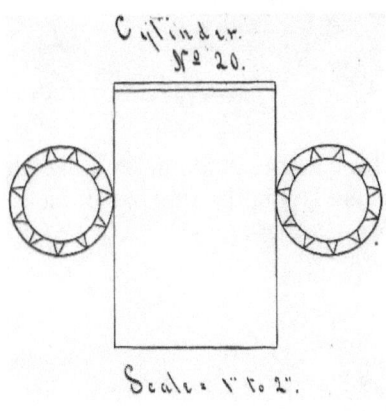

Cylinder. N° 20.

Scale 1" to 2".

47

Place the paper so that the long edges are parallel with the front of desk; bisect the back edge, and place a point four inches directly in front of it which shall be the center of a three inch horizontal line; draw the line; this line shall be the upper edge of an oblong three by five inches; draw the oblong.

On the right and left sides of oblong place points one-fourth inch from the upper edge; join opposite points.

Bisect the right and left sides of oblong; join these points with a ruler and place points one inch to the right and one inch to the left of oblong; with last points as centers describe two one and one-half inch circles and two two-inch circles.

Beginning at any point in the circumferences of inner circles divide them into one-fourth inch spaces; every other space in the circumference shall be the base of an isosceles triangle, whose apex touches the outer circle: draw the triangles.

Transfer to the scale of one to two. Cut, crease, fold and glue.

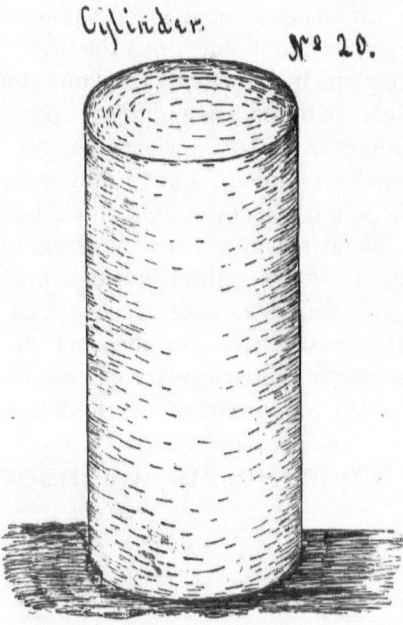

Cylinder.   № 20.

A cylinder of wood three inches in diameter and eight inches long should be provided for rolling and gluing the side of cylinder.

Model No. 21. - Cone

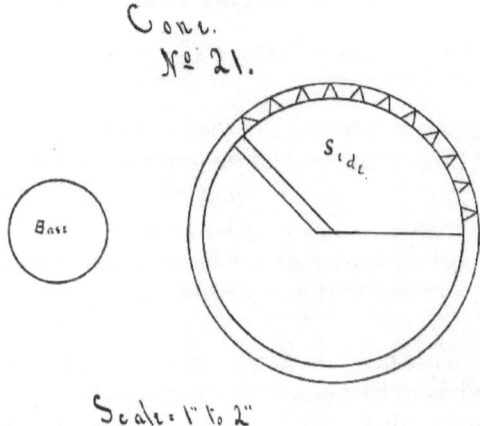

Place the paper so that the long edges are parallel with the front of desk; find the center of paper; with this point as a center draw a four-inch circle, and a four and one-half inch circle; place ruler in position to draw the horizontal diameters, and draw a radius of inner circle to the right; in line with diameters and two inches to the left of outer circle place a point, which shall be the center of a one and one-half inch circle; draw the circle.

Cut out a circular plinth of card-board equal to the last circle; place a point on card-board on the outer edge of circle; place the plinth in a vertical position so that the last point shall rest on the right end of radius of inner circle; roll the plinth upward along the circumference of the inner circle until the point in plinth again rests upon the circumference of inner circle; join this point in the circumference with the center.

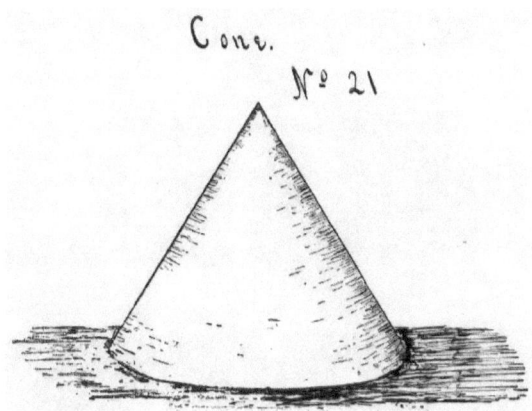

Construct a one-fourth inch margin on the left side of this segment; construct isosceles triangles between the circumferences as in the cylinder.

Transfer to a scale of one to two. Cut, crease, fold and glue.

49

Series Three - Useful Articles in Cardboard

The object of this series is to place in the hands of teachers, - who cannot obtain permission, time, place, tools or material for teaching wood-work, - a series of Manual Training lessons that may be practically followed in any school-room. The series is also an excellent preparation for introducing the pupils to the real working drawings needed in advanced work in wood and iron. Thus, when they come to the higher work, they will have a very fair idea of what is needed.

The drawings as in the preceding work, are for the help of teachers, who can make their models from them. The pupils should be taught to make drawings from these models; then models from their drawings.

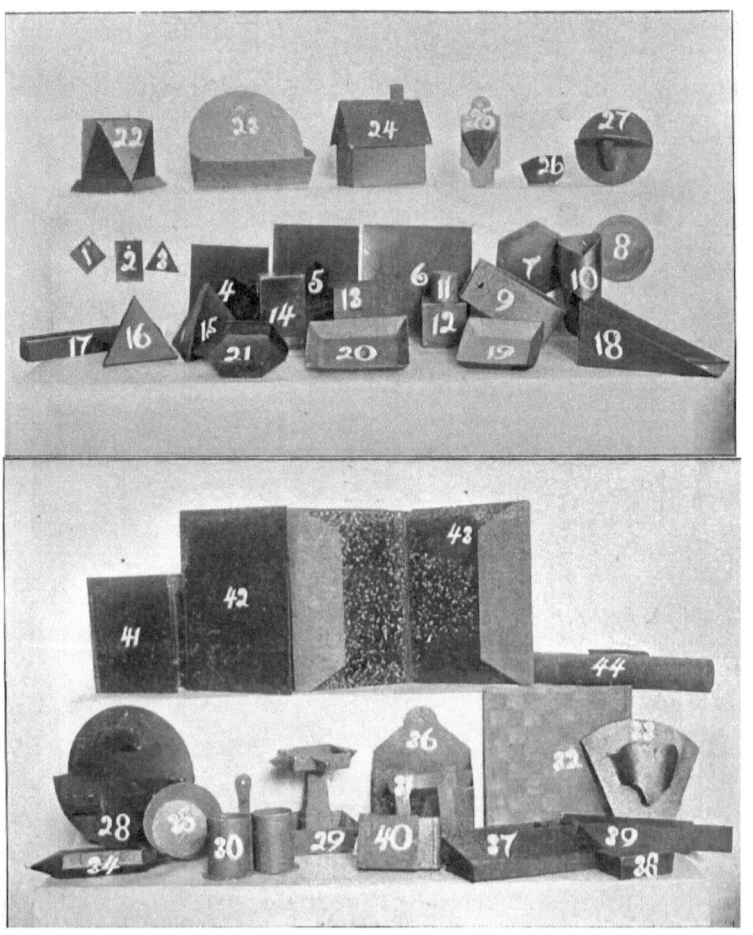

Tools and Material Needed

A good quality of straw board, three or four times as thick as a postal-card; some leatherette paper for the outside covers of the portfolio, music-roll, card-cases, boxes, etc.; some prettily figured paper, such as may be found on the fly leaf of some books, for the outside and inside of card receivers, mats, work-boxes, comb-cases, etc., and for the inside of portfolios; some thin pale blue and red paper for the inside of boxes, music-rolls, card-receivers, etc.; Le Page's Liquid Glue for gluing card-board; and some bookbinder's paste. The tools used are the same as those used in the preceding work, with the addition of a small paste-brush.

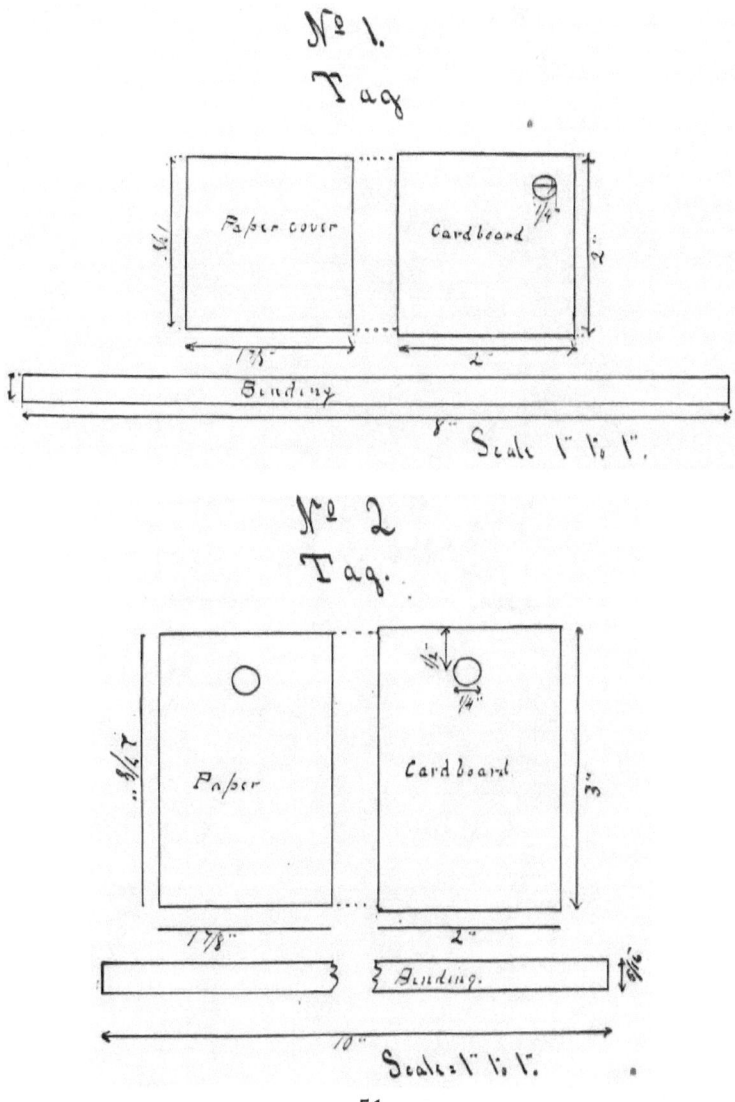

51

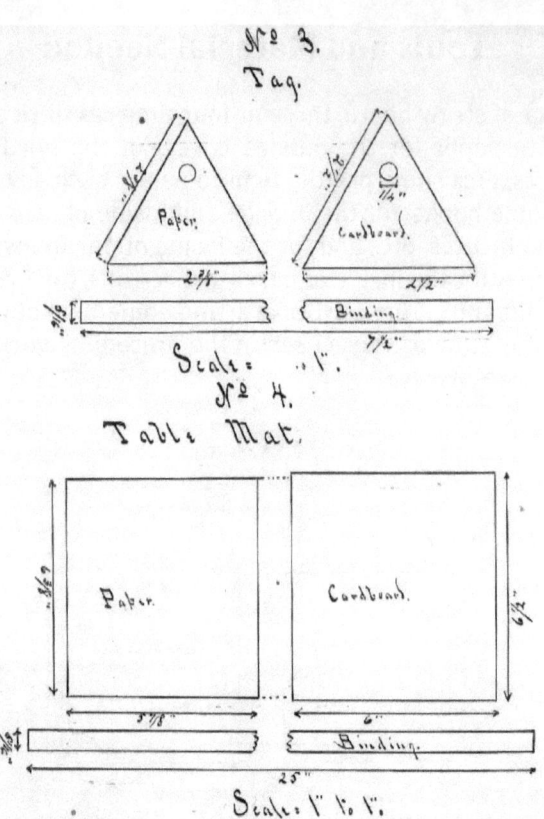

Nº 3.
Tag.

Paper.   Cardboard.
2¾"   2½"

¾"   Binding
7½"

Scale: ¼ to 1".

Nº 4.
Table Mat.

Paper.   Cardboard.

3⅞"   6"

Binding.

25"

Scale 1" to 1".

Nº 5.
Table Mat.

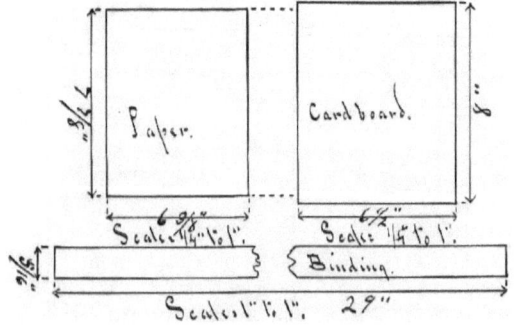

Paper.   Cardboard.

6¼"   6½"

Scale ¼" to 1".   Scale ¼" to 1".

Binding.

Scale 1" to 1".   29"

52

Nº 6.
Table Mat.

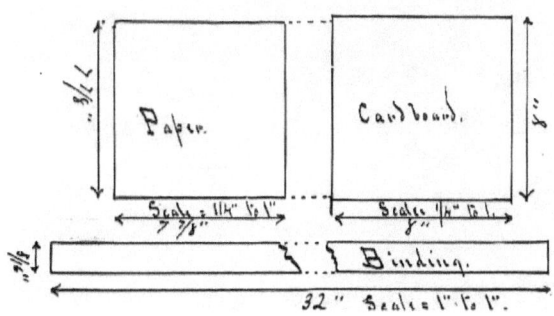

Paper.

Cardboard.

Scale = 1¼" to 1"
7 ⅜"

Scale = ¼" to 1.
8"

Binding.

32" Scale = 1" to 1".

Nº 7.
Table Mat.

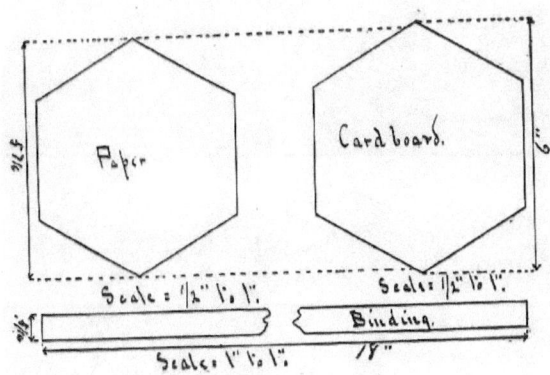

Paper

Cardboard.

Scale = ½" to 1".

Scale = ½" to 1".

Binding.

Scale = 1" to 1".   18"

Nº 8.
Table Mat.

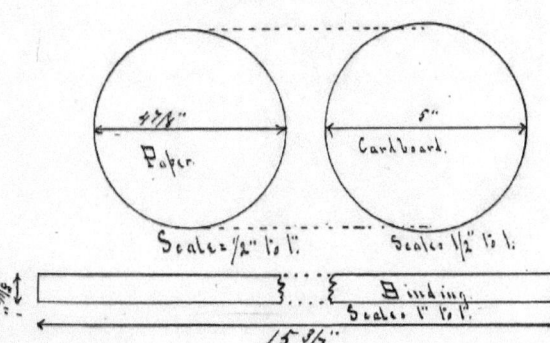

4⅞"

5"

Paper.

Cardboard.

Scale = ½" to 1".

Scale = ½" to 1.

Binding.
Scale = 1" to 1".

15 ⅜"

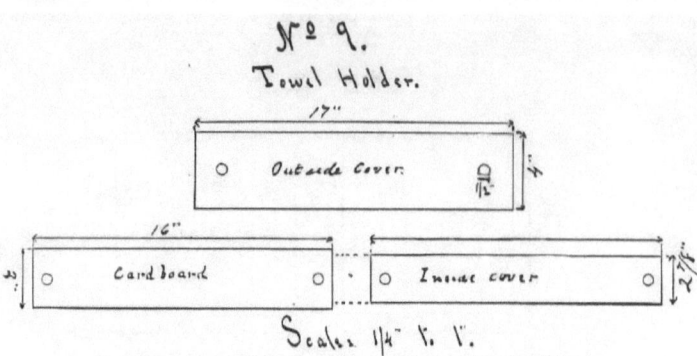

Nº 9.

Towel Holder.

Scales 1/4" to 1'.

Fig. Nº 2 Showing process of
pasting on ornamental covers,
on models from Nº 9. up.

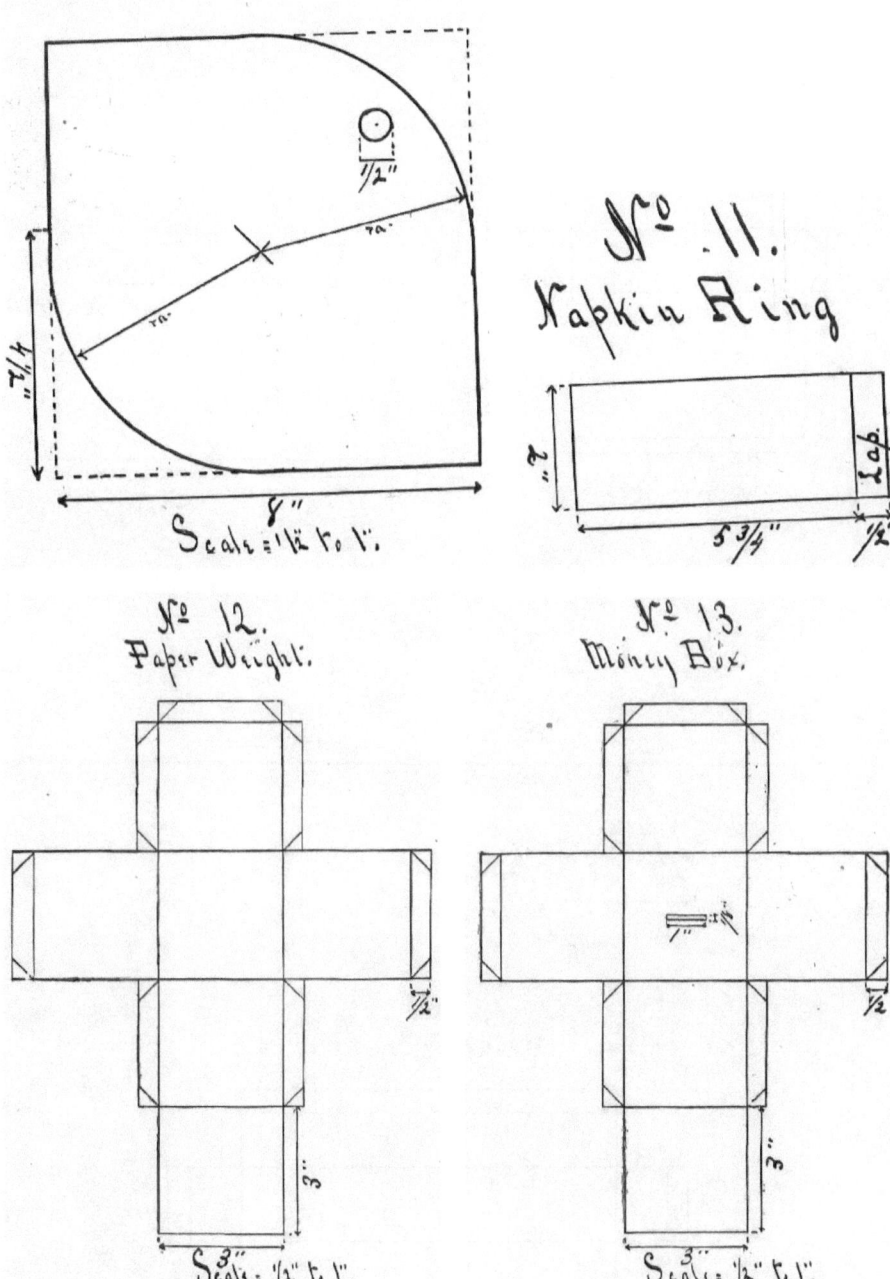

Nº 10
Feather Duster Holder.

½"
ra.
ra.
7½"
8"
Scale: 1½" to 1".

Nº 11.
Napkin Ring

2"
Lap.
5¾"
½"

Nº 12.
Paper Weight.

½"
3"
Scale: ½" to 1".

Nº 13.
Money Box.

½
3"
Scale: ½" to 1".

№. 14.
Paper Weight

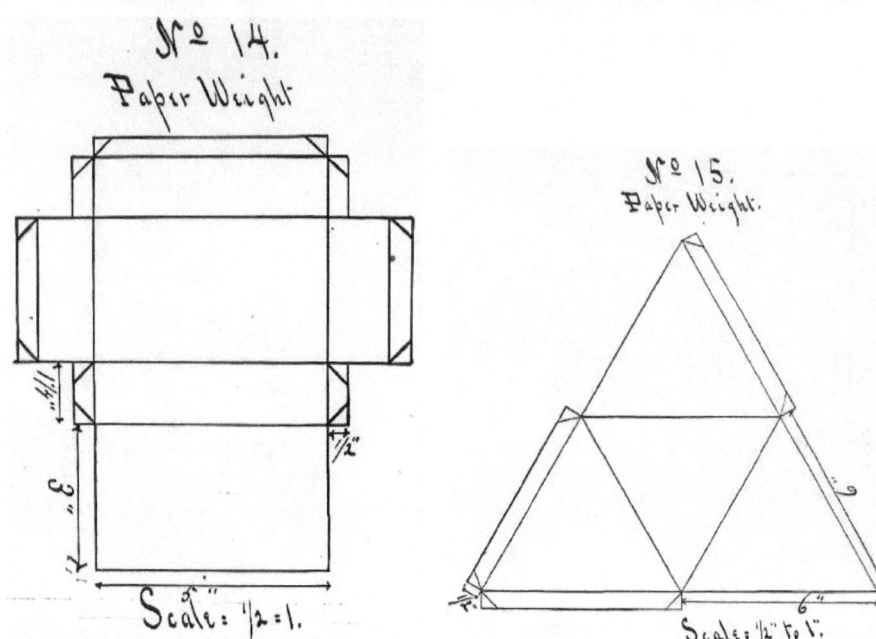

1½" 3" ½"

Scale: ½ = 1.

№. 15.
Paper Weight.

6" 6"

Scale: ½" to 1".

№. 16
Watch Stand.

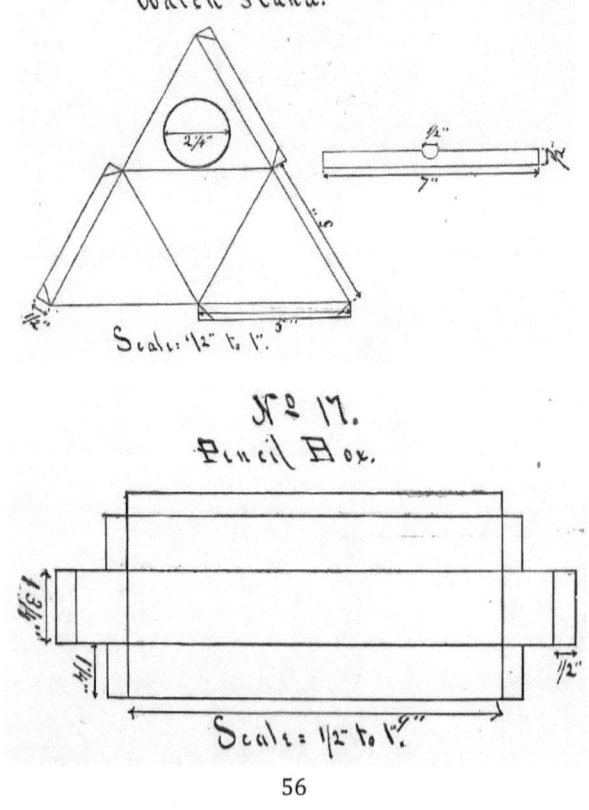

2¼"

½" 7" ½"

Scale: ½" to 1".

№. 17.
Pencil Box.

1¾" 1¼" ½"

Scale: ½" to 1".

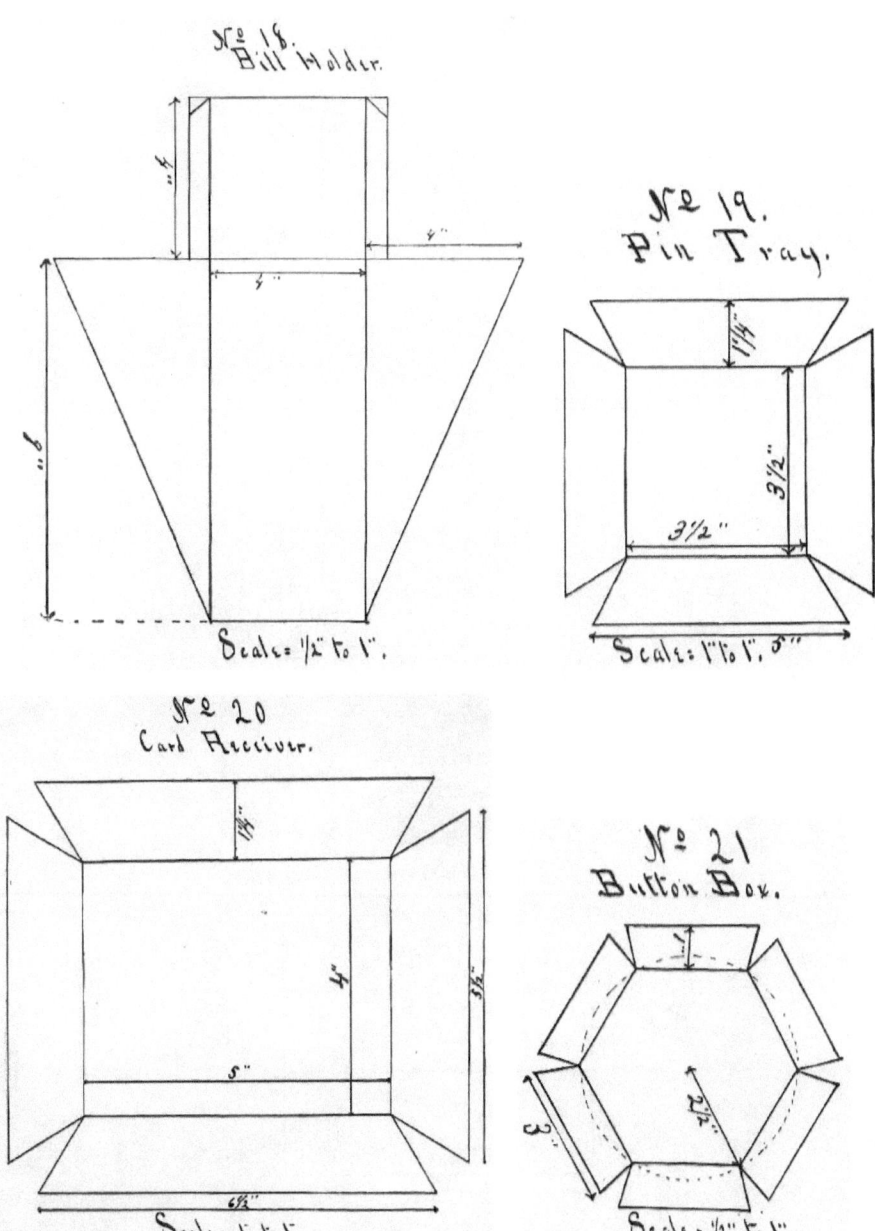

Nº 18.
Bill Holder.

4"
6"
4"
4"
Scale = ½" to 1".

Nº 19.
Pin Tray.

1¼"
3½"
3½"
Scale = 1" to 1". 5"

Nº 20
Card Receiver.

1¼"
4"
5"
3½"
6½"
Scale = 1" to 1".

Nº 21
Button Box.

1"
2½"
3"
Scale = ½" to 1".

57

Nº 22.
Work Box

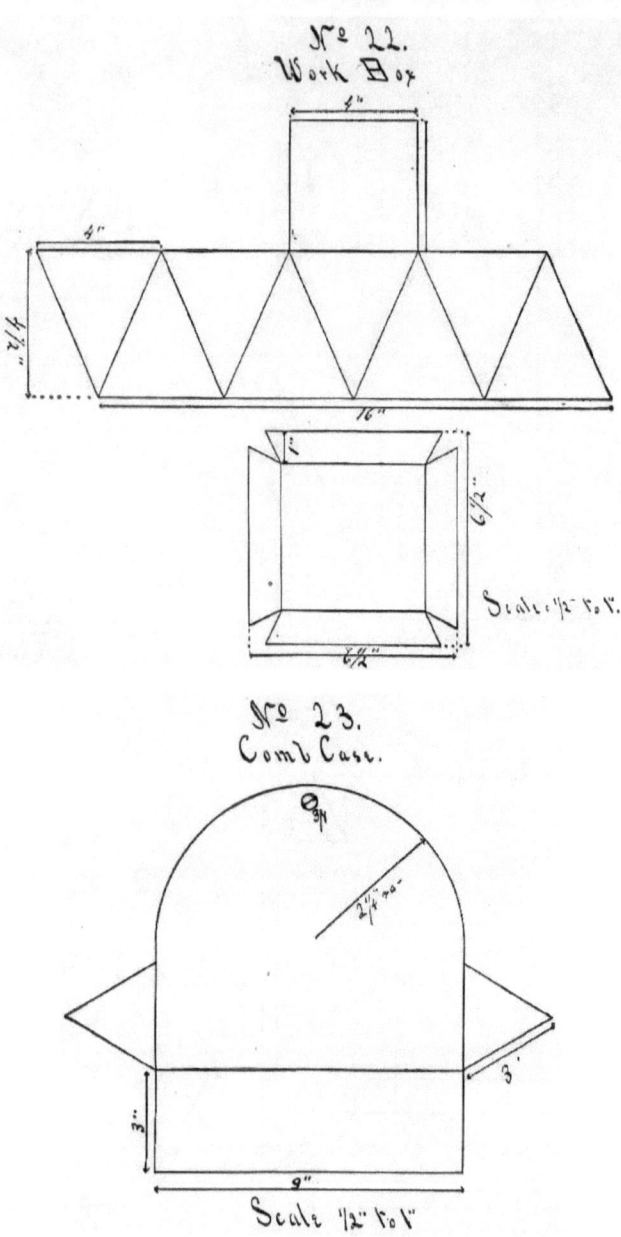

Scale ½" to 1'.

Nº 23.
Comb Case.

Scale ½" to 1'.

Bank

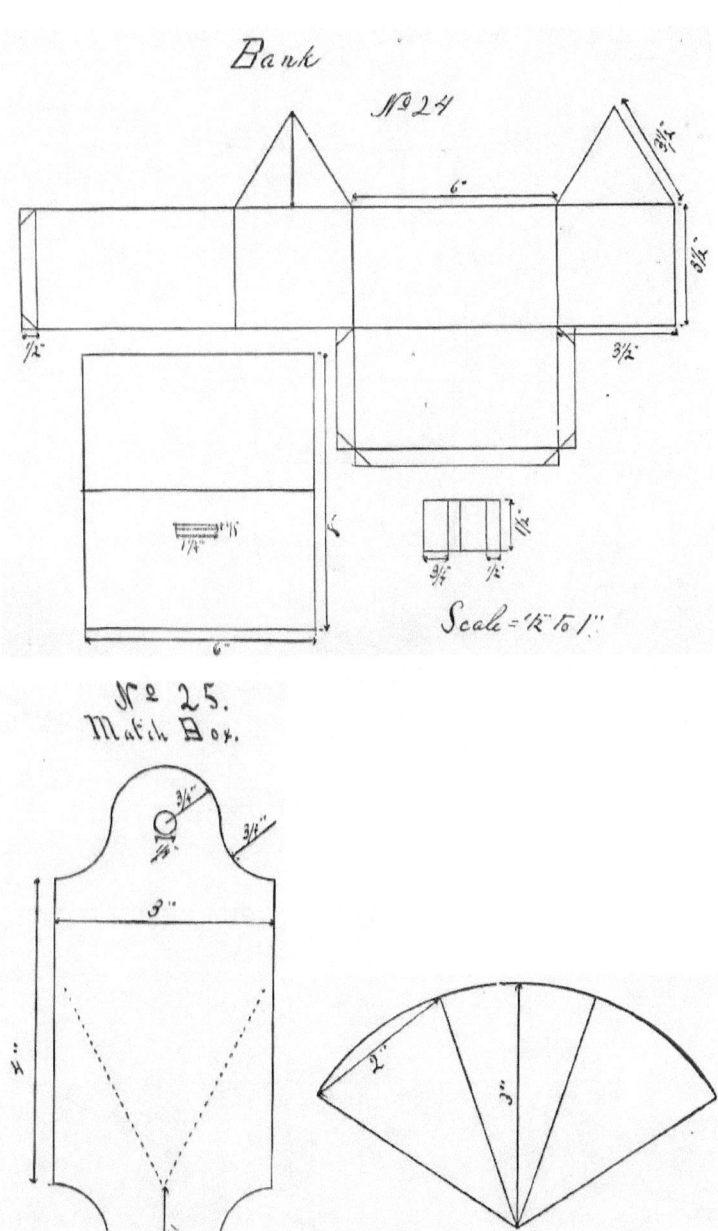

No 24

6"

3½"

3½"

3½"

½"

3½"

1½"

1¾"

6"

¾" ½"

Scale = ½" to 1"

No 25.
Match Box.

3½"

¾"

¼"

3½"

3"

4"

2"

3"

Scale: 1" to 1".

N⁰ 26.
Match Box.

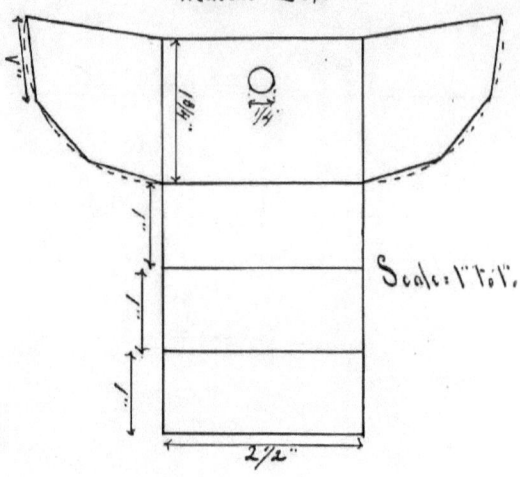

Scale: 1" to 1".

2½"

Wall bracket.
N⁰ 27

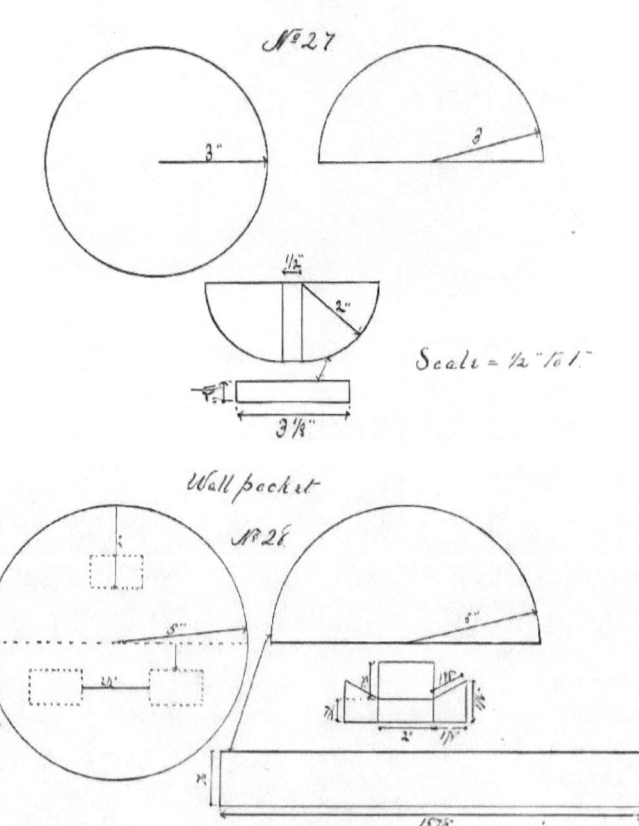

3"

3

½"

2"

Scale = ½" to 1."

3⅛"

Wall pocket
N⁰ 28.

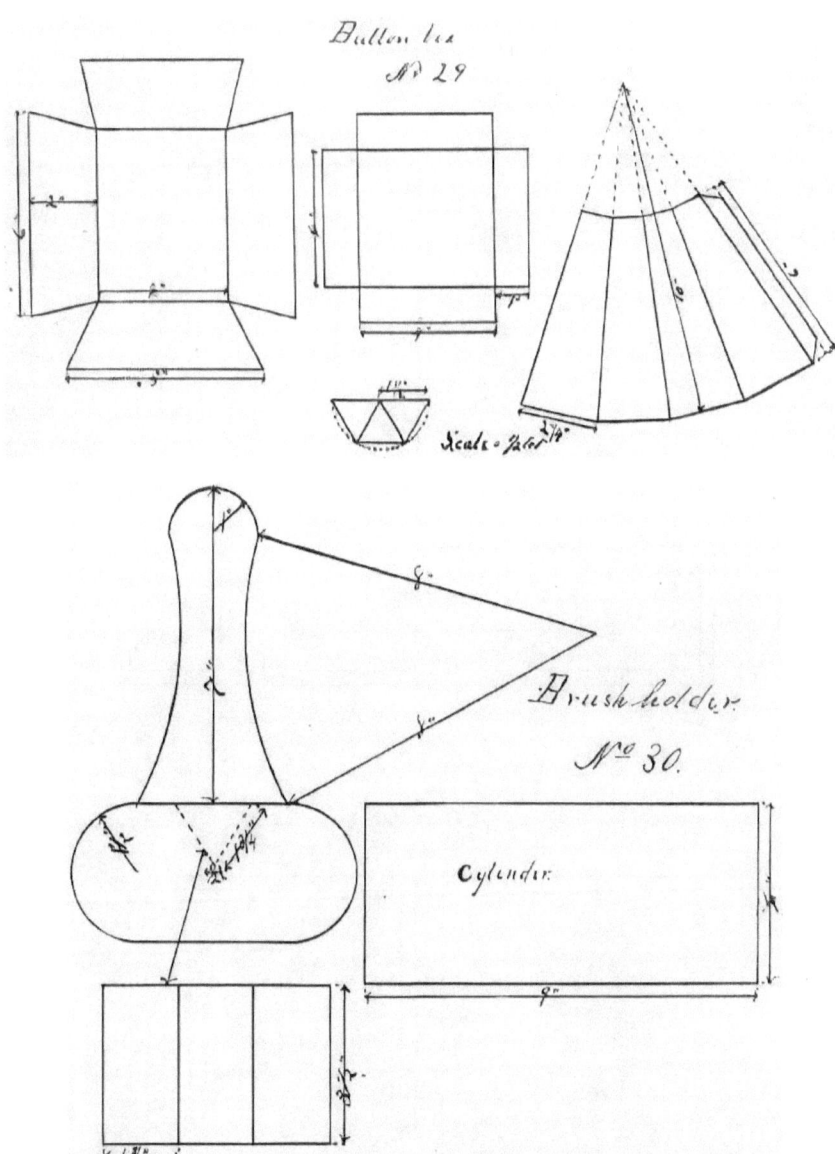

Bullen tea
№ 29

Scale = ½ Feet

Brush holder.
№ 30.

Cylinder.

61

Picture frame

N.º 31

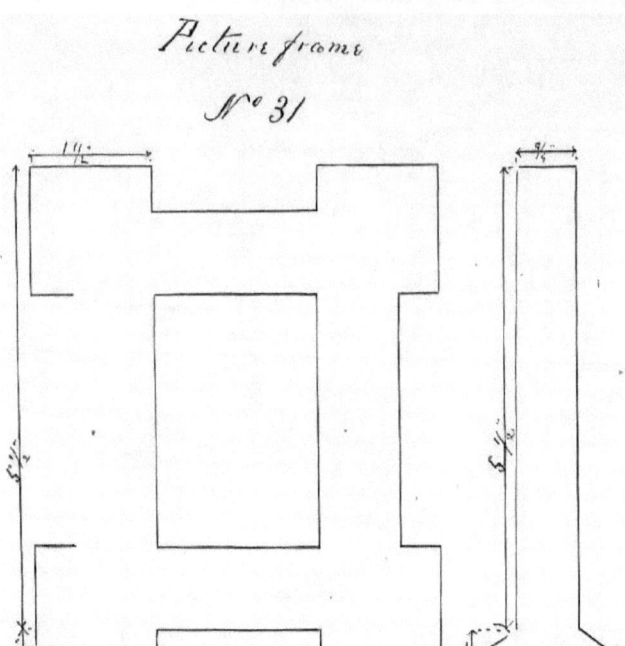

Scale = 1" to 1"

Checkerboard.

N.º 32

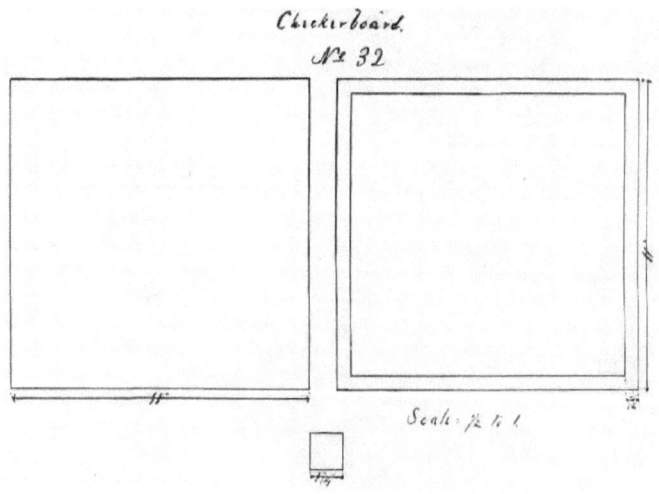

Scale: ½ to 1

Broom holder
№ 33

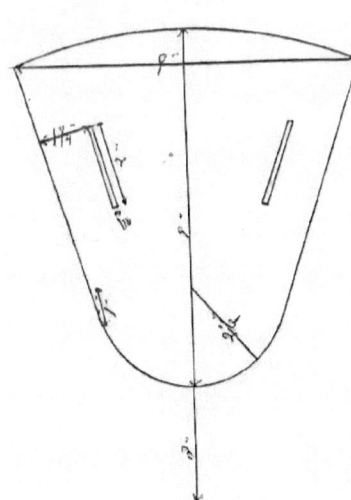
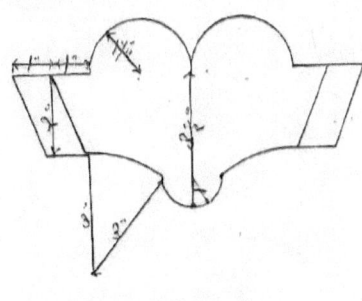

Scale = ½" to 1"

Key-hanger
№ 34

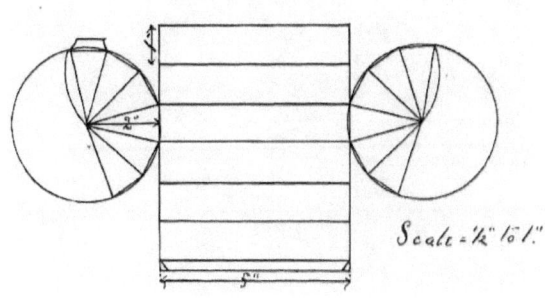

Scale = ½" to 1."

Thread-box

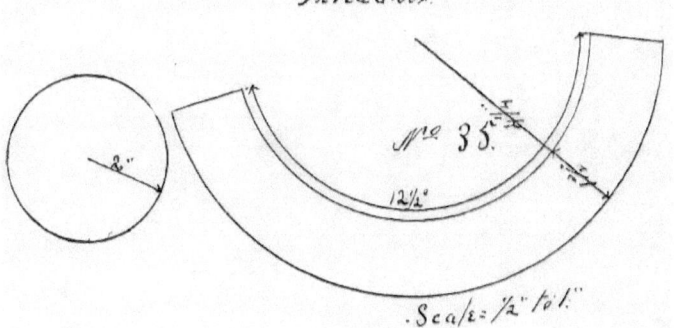

№ 35.

12½"

Scale = ½" to 1."

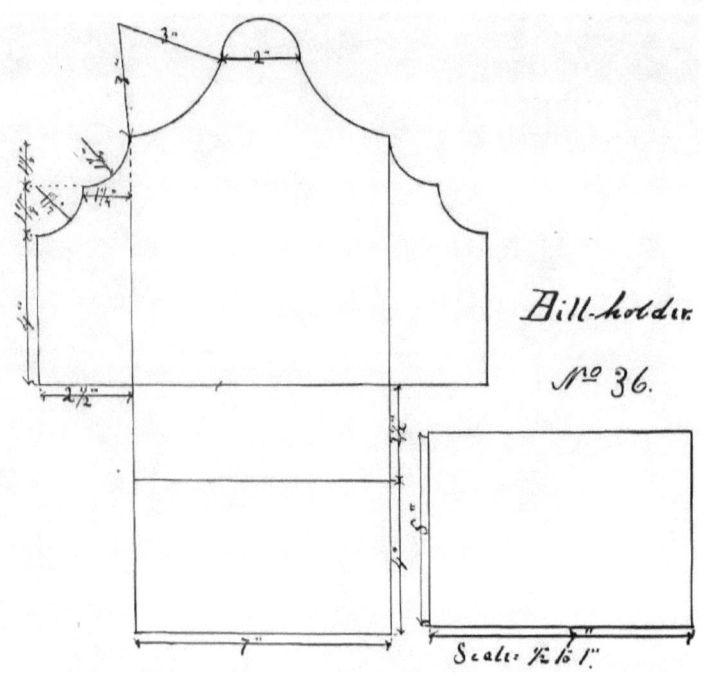

Bill-holder.

Nº 36.

Scale: ½ to 1".

Pen tray.

Nº 37

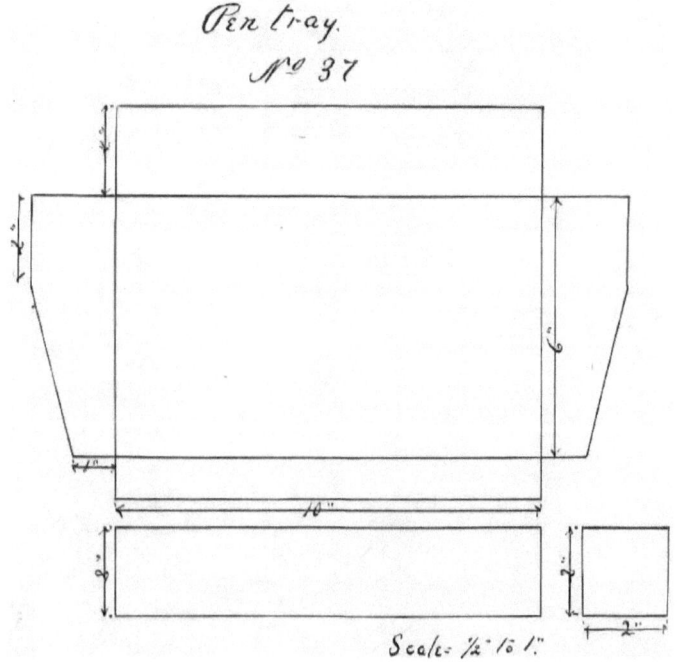

Scale: ½ to 1".

Box
№ 38.

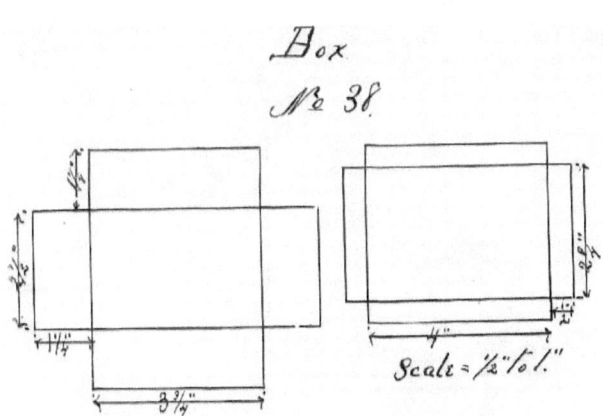

Scale = ½" to 1."

Pencil box
№ 39.

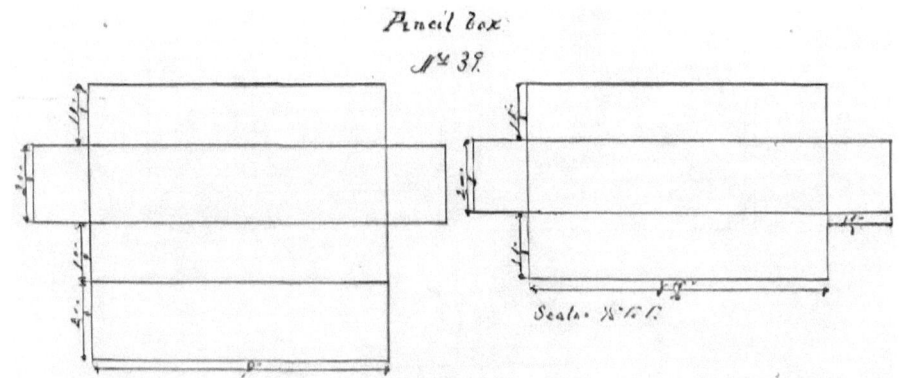

Scale = ⅛" to 1."

Cardcase.
№ 40.

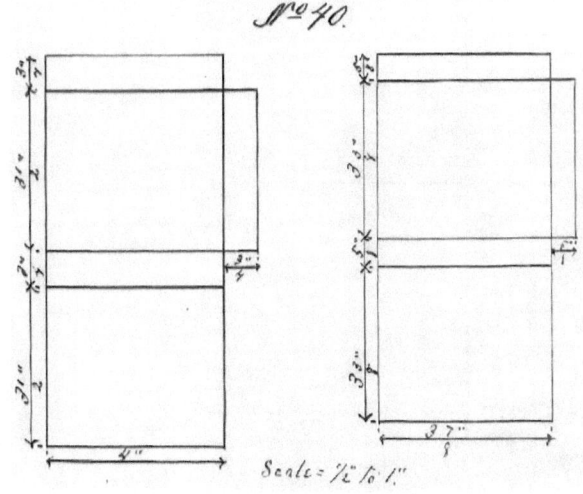

Scale = ½" to 1."

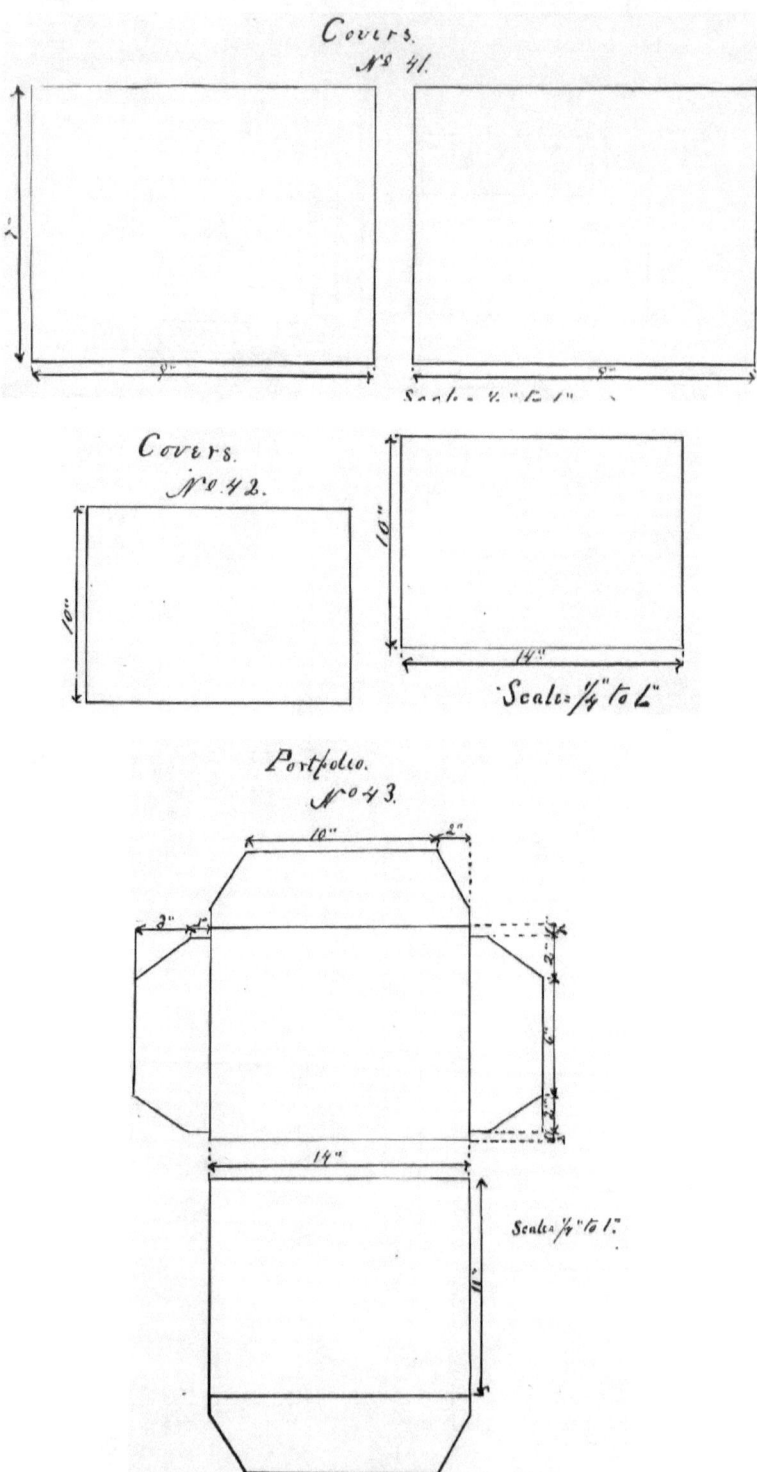

Covers.
N⁰ 41.

Covers.
N⁰ 42.

Scale ¼" to 1"

Portfolio.
N⁰ 43.

Scale ¼" to 1"

Music case.

N.º 44

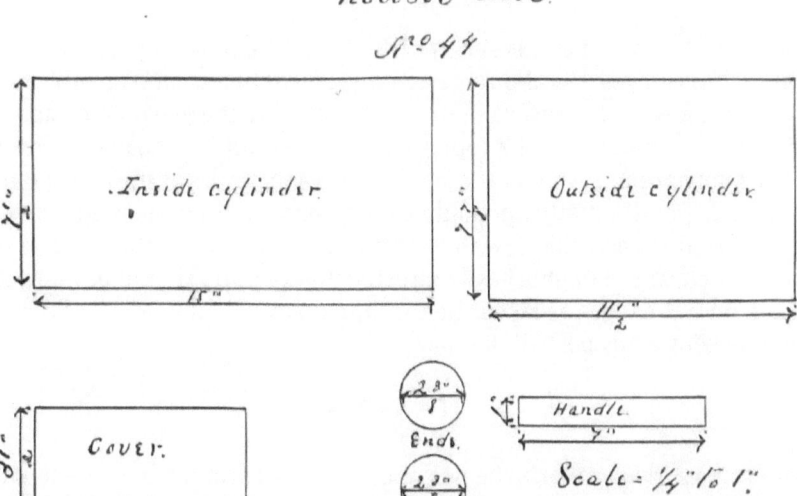

Inside cylinder.

7½"

15"

Outside cylinder.

7½"

11½"

Cover.

3½"

5½"

Ends.

Handle.

5"

Scale = ¼" to 1".

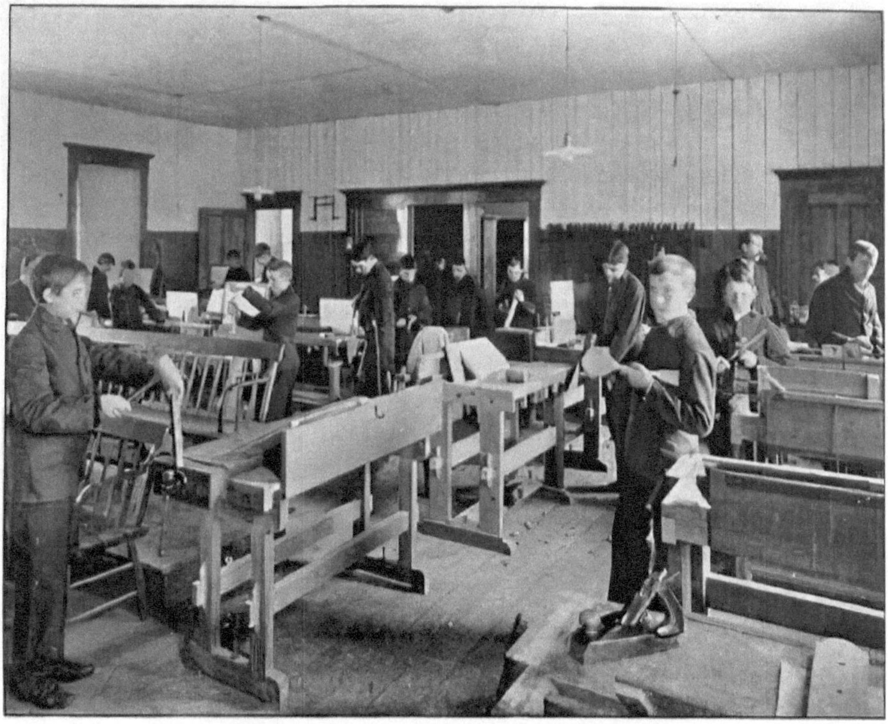

Series Four

The work embodied in this series of models is the most important of all to the pupil. Eleven years is about the average age of pupils who are able to begin it, but it would not be right to say that all of that age would be able to do the work, nor would it be proper to exclude all pupils who are under that age, for many are more apt at the age of nine than others at the age of fourteen. This depends greatly upon inheritance, natural brightness and environment. At this particular age character is easily moulded; the hand and eye easily trained, and thoughts easily directed. Every pupil should be allowed to proceed with the work as fast as he can, and do excellent work, for every one should be kept at his best all the time.

The Work

With this particular work, the possibilities for all around development are greater than in any other form of Manual Training, therefore it is the best form for public school work. In it there are a greater number of healthful exercises taught than are embodied in any other work. There are no harmful exercises.

The articles made are such as to embody the exercises in the order of their simplicity, and can be so arranged as to fit the daily growth of the pupil.

With careful teaching of the use of tools there is a natural tendency towards neatness and accuracy, which cannot be said of all kinds of work that could be used for manual training purposes.

It brings a pupil face to face with himself, and he sees his weaknesses and his good qualities as he never saw them before.

These elements of character which Manual Training should develop, such as independence, order, neatness, respect for the dignity of intelligent labor and a love for work in general, are fundamentally established, and there is an awakening of a lively interest in all subjects that pertain to scientific and skillful work and thought. Another important fact is, that one becomes more generally skillful in this work than in any other, and the exercises performed are fundamental in teaching and performing all other kinds of work that could be used for manual training purposes and which should follow this.

The Tools

The knife is the tool with which more articles can be made than with any other, hence a greater number of exercises can be performed with it. It is also more universally known and used than any other tool.

If any one makes an article with a knife, he can claim that the work was solely his own, for the tool was held and guided by his own hand, and the eye was exercised in judging of surfaces and curves; but when he makes an article, using the plane where a knife could have been used, he can claim but part of the work as his own, for the cutting blade of the plane was held and guided to a great extent by the stock of the plane. This is why the knife is the fundamental tool in Sloyd work.

Messrs. Chandler and Barber, 17 Eliot St., Boston, Mass., have with great care prepared a bench and a full list of tools, which are recognized by all teachers as the best that can be had and arc sold at a very small profit.

Never use a poor tool, and always keep tools in excellent cutting condition. Never attempt to teach the use of them until you have learned to do it readily yourself.

Use tools of common size; for boys who are old enough to do the work are able to handle the ordinary tools, and they are more steady in the hands than smaller ones.

The following tools should be kept at every bench: a knife, a jack-plane, a smoothing-plane, a marking-gauge, a tri-square, a two foot rule (in one piece), a pair of steel compasses and a pencil.

All the other tools except the cross-cut and splitting-saws should be kept in a cabinet with a glass front, with slanting shelves and apartments for each tool. The cross-cut and splitting-saws should be hung on a rack near where the sawing is done, and all tools that are not at the benches should be given out by the teacher or some pupil appointed for the office. The grindstone, chopping-block and saw-horses should be in a place where they will be out of the way of the benches.

For the drawing the *Milton Bradley* kit is the best in the market and serves the purpose very well.

Six sets of good drawing instruments are enough for a class of twenty-five. They should be given out by the teacher and kept with the paper at his desk. Sand-paper should be used as sparingly as possible and should be given out by the teacher. Grades No. 1 1-2 and 1-2 are the best for the purpose.

After the general instruction has been given to the class, individual teaching should be given in the sharpening, care, and use of the tools.

Seats for the class should be arranged in front of the teacher's bench and drawing board, where he can perform exercises that can be as well taught in class as with individual instruction.

All tools should be kept dry, no rust being allowed to corrode them. During the vacation months they should be wiped with oiled waste, wrapped in oiled paper, packed in cases, and put in a dry place.

Any first class carpenter or cabinet-maker can give to a teacher all necessary instruction in the sharpening, use and care of the tools.

Material

It has been found through years of experience and careful observation that wood is best adapted for work in Manual Training for pupils in the upper

Grammar grades. It can be easily obtained, it offers the right amount of resistance to the tools and hand; the pupils become interested in finding where the different woods grow, and the study of the nature, growth and general appearance of trees gives a basis for the study of design.

In the analysis of this series the different kinds of wood that are best adapted for the work are given.

Great care should be used to select wood of the best quality, straight grain, good color, kiln-dried; and when selecting white-wood take that which is free from sap. It is a good plan to purchase enough at one time to last a year, if it can be stored in a dry place.

The Room

Many ask if this kind of Manual Training can not be taught in an ordinary school-room, and the work done on a common school desk. This, however, is not practical.

A special room on the lower floor or in the basement, if dry, is the best place for the work. The room should be at least thirty feet square and well lighted from opposite sides.

In setting the benches plenty of room should be allowed for passage ways, for the sawing of lumber, and enough between benches so that the pupils need not come in contact with each other while working.

It is very desirable to have black-boards around the room, for drawings explanatory of the construction of plane figures, descriptions of parts of tools, positions of the body while working, etc.

Mention has already been made of the seats arranged in front of the teacher's bench and black-board. This is a very important feature and much good teaching can be done on account of it which could not be done as well in any other way.

The teacher should meet his class here at least once a week to talk over with them the work in general, to lecture on woods, tools, etc., and to explain different exercises with the tools and instruments.

A cabinet should be provided for the teacher's models, and in a side room, fitted with broad shelves, should be placed the finished work of the pupils. In another room there should be lockers for each pupil arranged in sections, each section to contain twenty-four lockers. A convenient size for each locker is twenty-two inches in height, ten inches in width and fourteen inches in depth. One door can serve for three lockers. These should contain the pupil's drawing kit, suit and unfinished work. These lockers are an important feature, for it helps in a great degree to teach neatness and order.

The Models

The teacher in Manual Training should consult with the teacher in design, and be careful that the models from which the pupils work are articles of real worth, beautiful in shape. Many practical persons who have artistic tastes rightly criticize the models which are used in many Manual Training Schools. Other persons, disregarding the necessary and fundamental exercises in making the objects, would simply teach ornamentation. This, however, is a wrong impression for pupils to form of what is most valuable in an object. Again there are those who go to the other extreme. Some would have no ornamentation at all, not even on useful parts, while others would over-ornament to the extent of sacrificing useful parts.

There is, however, a happy medium, which can be maintained by ornamenting useful parts, making them none the less useful but more beautiful.

Never make a model ugly in shape for the sake of teaching an exercise. It would be better to go on to the next model and in the meantime invent something useful and pretty to contain that exercise.

Finally, there should be a variety of shapes, and in the series there should be a number of models having such convex surfaces as are most graceful and cannot be made with instruments in a mechanical way but must be drawn and made free hand. This might be called modeling in wood. It tests and educates the eye and hand in a wonderful degree.

Marking

This is one of the most difficult tasks that a teacher has to perform. It is sometimes hard to decide how to mark. The teacher is supposed to know, all the time, the quality and amount of work that is being done on each model on which the class is working, and as he passes from bench to bench he can so watch the work that he can easily pass his judgment on the workmanship and faithfulness of the pupil. Teachers have to accept work from some pupils that he would not accept from others. For instance, here is a boy who has inherited a strong tendency towards skillfulness in the use of tools, and it is quite easy for him to do the work in an excellent manner, but he should be kept at his very best all the time and show steady improvement. The duty of the teacher, here, would be to make the right sort of a leader of him, encouraging him to do extra work in the way of invention, and helping to teach those who need special instruction.

Here is another pupil who is naturally dull and has inherited no tendency towards skillfulness. It would be impossible for him to equal the other in his work, but if he has done his best after having been shown his deficiencies and has made another trial, his work should be accepted, even if not up to the standard of excellence that the average pupil can make.

Lectures and Reference Books

The teacher's work should by no means be confined to teaching the use of tools and making models. The lectures that he gives should interest his pupils in the study of the history of tools, and the nature, use and manufacture of metals. This will lead to a closer study of General History, Literature, Geography, Geology, and Physics.

He should be able to refer his pupils to books upon these subjects, and in class have them relate what they have found. Great care should be taken in teaching the correct positions of the body while handling the tools, and illustrating how the body is developed by right exercises and injured by wrong exercises.

General Hints

Never try to help a pupil by doing his work for him.

A period of two hours twice a week will keep the class interested and the hand will not forget from one period to another.

The benches and tools should be inspected before and after each lesson.

The models should be given to those who have made them, at the close of the school year.

Keep plenty of good surgeon's plaster and bandages on hand, for accidents with the knife are likely to happen.

When a certain degree of excellency has been reached by the pupils, let them ornament some of the later models with appropriate designs of wood carving. Encourage pupils to have tools and a bench of their own.

The best way to proceed with the work is to have the pupils make a working drawing from the teacher's model, and then from that drawing make his model.

A good way to examine the pupils would be to show them the new exercise that is contained in their next model and let them invent a model embodying that exercise, making the working drawing of it first; or the teacher could make a drawing of the next model and have the pupil work from it. This could be done once or twice during the year.

Model No. 1. - Glove Mender

Prepare for the class pieces of wood 1" wide, and 8' long sawed from a 7-8" board. On one of the 1" sides, which should be marked No. 1, draw a line, with the aid of a ruler, along the edge of the wood, 1-8" from the side. With the knife, cut this side down to the line drawn, making it square to No. 1. Mark this side No. 2. On side No. 2 draw a line that shall be 9-16" from side No. 1. Cut to this line, making the side square to No. 2. Mark this side No. 3.

On side No. 3 draw a line that shall be 9-16" from side No. 2. Cut down to this line, making the side square to No. 3. Mark this side No. 4.

With the use of the tri-square draw a line around the stick 1-2" from one end. Cut off the end of the stick at this line making the end square to all the side faces. Draw a line around the stick 6 1-16" from this end. Cut off the stick at this line, square to all the side faces, making a square prism 9-16" x 6 1-16". Draw lines around the stick 1-4" from one of the ends and 3-16" from the other end, and, using these as guide lines, draw the plan (omitting the curves) upon two opposite sides of the wood. Cut the other two opposite sides down to the lines of the drawing, then draw plan upon these two sides. Cut down to these lines, making a frustrum of a square pyramid.

Quadrisect all edges of both ends and join opposite points except the middle points. Cut all corners to lines, making the frustrum of an octagonal pyramid. Round all corners, making the frustrum of a cone. Draw lines around the stick 1-4" from the larger end and 3-16" from the smaller end. Round the ends according to the drawing.

Finish with coarse and fine sand-paper. If the model is too long, cut from the smaller end.

Model No. 2. - Seed Stick

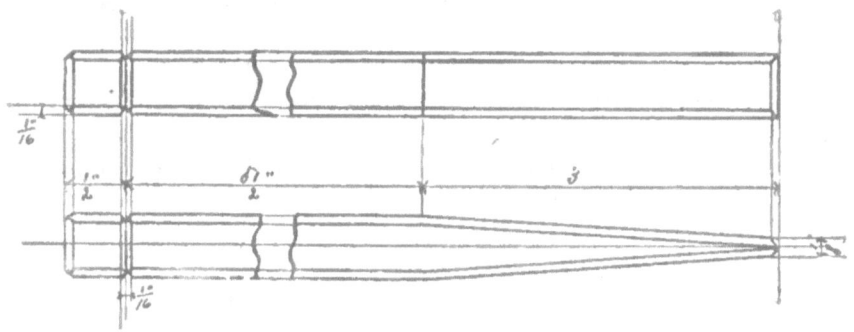

FULL SIZE.

Prepare pieces of wood 1" wide and 10" long, sawed from a 7-8" board.

Make an oblong 17-32" x 9 1-16", using the plane on the side faces and the knife on the end faces, following the same rules in lining, cutting, and squaring as in model No. 1.

Draw lines around the stick 1-2" from one end and 3" from the other end. Draw the plan upon two opposite sides of the stick. Cut the notches with a knife, and also to the oblique lines.

Place the stick with one corner uppermost in the vice, bevel the four longer edges with the plane: with the knife bevel the edges on the oblique sides and on the ends.

By wrapping sand-paper around a small square block finish up the ends first, then the oblique sides and then the remaining sides. If the model is too long, cut from the smaller end.

Model No. 3. - Round Flower Stick

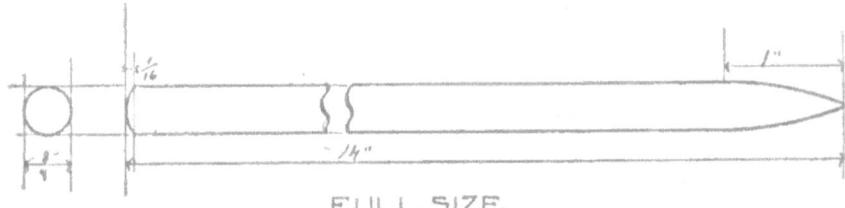

FULL SIZE.

Prepare pieces of wood 3-4" wide and 15" long, sawed from a 7-8" board.

With the use of the knife and proceding as in model No. 1 cut the stick to an oblong 7-16" x 15".

Draw a line around the stick 1-4" from one of the ends.

Place the stick horizontally in the vice and with the cross-cut saw cut the stick off 1-16" outside this line. Square the end with a knife up to this line.

Draw a line around the stick 14 1-16" from the end. Cut off the end at this line, proceeding as with the other end.

Quadrisect all edges of both ends and join opposite points.

Cut all corners to lines making an octagonal prism. Round all corners, making a cylinder.

Draw lines around the stick 1-16" from one end and 1' from the other end. Round these ends according to the drawing.

Model No. 4. - Letter Opener

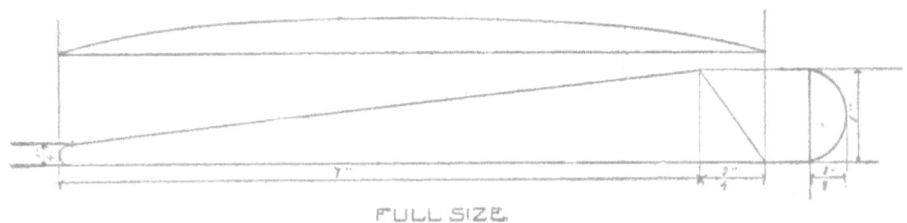

FULL SIZE.

Prepare pieces of wood 1 1-4" wide by 9" long, sawed from a 3-4" board.

Plane to an oblong 7-16" x 1 1-16" x 9", using the marking gauge for lines instead of the pencil and ruler.

Cut off both ends as in the preceding models, using the point of the knife for lines instead of the pencil, making an oblong 7-16" x 1 1-16" x 8 1-8".

74

Draw the plan upon one of the sides of the stick. Cut off end with tenon-saw up to 1-16" of the short oblique line. Cut with knife up to this line and to remaining lines.

Place the elevation drawing upon two opposite sides of the wood and cut to lines. Model with knife according to end view, and finish with sand-paper.

Model No. 5. - Square Flower Stick

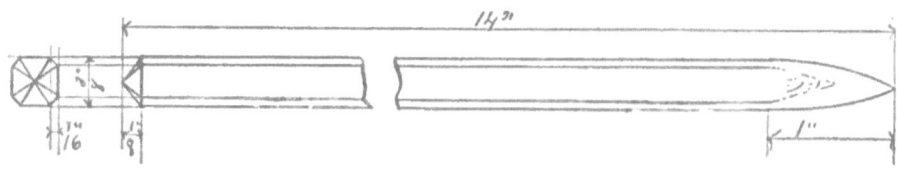

Have the pupils saw from a 7-8" board a piece 3-4" x 15". Plane this piece to an oblong 13-32" x 15". Square both ends with saw and knife making an oblong 13-32" x 14 1-16".

Draw lines around the stick 1-8" from one end and 1" from the other. Place stick with one corner uppermost between the jaws of the vice and bevel the edges with the plane.

Cut ends with knife according to drawing and finish with sandpaper.

In all succeeding models the pupils should mark off and saw their own lumber.

Model No. 6. - File Handle

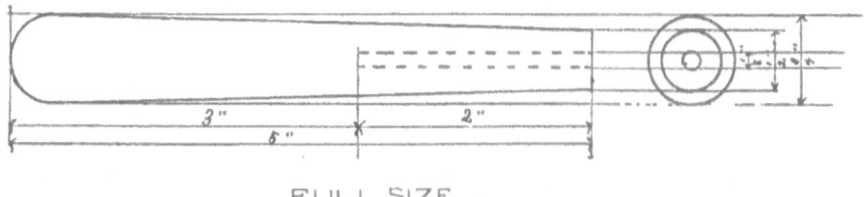

FULL SIZE.

Cut from a 7-8" board a piece 1" x 1". Plane this to an oblong 13-16" x 7". With the use of the tenon-saw and knife cut this to an oblong 13-16" x 5 1-16". Draw the diagonals on one end, and placing the stick in a vertical position in the vice, bore the hole with a pin-bit.

Draw the plan upon two opposite sides of the stick, omitting the curves. Cut with the knife to lines. Proceed in the same way with the remaining opposite sides, making the frustrum of a square pyramid.

Quadrisect the lines that are 1-4" from one end and all edges of the smaller end. Join opposite points and cut to lines, making the frustrum of an octagonal pyramid. Proceed with the rounding as in Model No. 1. Finish with file and sand-paper.

Model No. 7. - Key Label

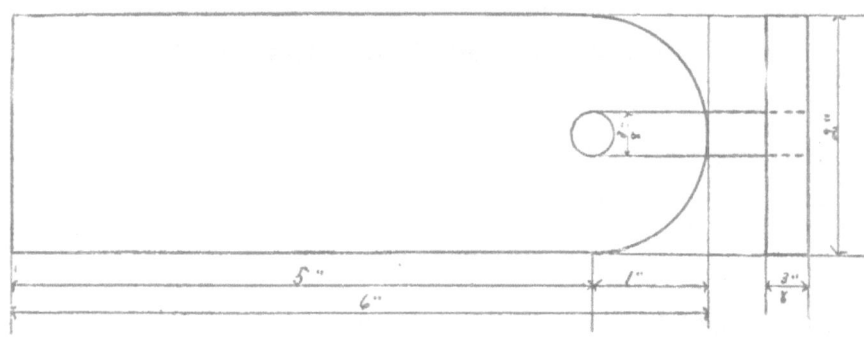

FULL SIZE.

Cut from a 1-2" board a piece 2 1-4" x 7", and from this prepare an oblong 13-32 x 2 1-32" x 6 1-32".

Draw the plan upon one of the sides of the wood. Bore hole with auger-bit. Cut to line with knife and finish with tile and sand-paper.

Model No. 8. - String Winder

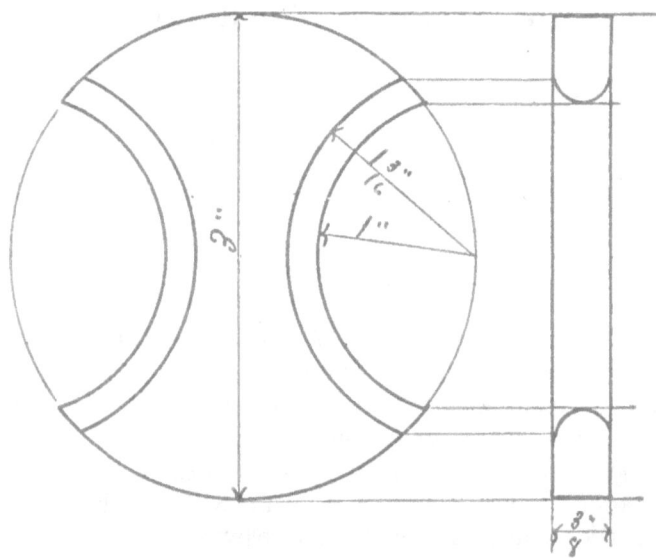

FULL SIZE.

Have the pupil cut from a 1-2" board a piece 4 1-8 x 4 1-8". Plane to size 13-32" x 4" x 4". Draw a line through the middle of this piece parallel with the grain of the wood. With the centre of this line for a centre, draw the plan upon the piece. Cut around with the turning-saw to within 1-16" of the outside the line. Cut with the knife up to the line. Round edges with the knife according to drawing and finish with tile and sand-paper.

Model No. 9. - Round Ruler

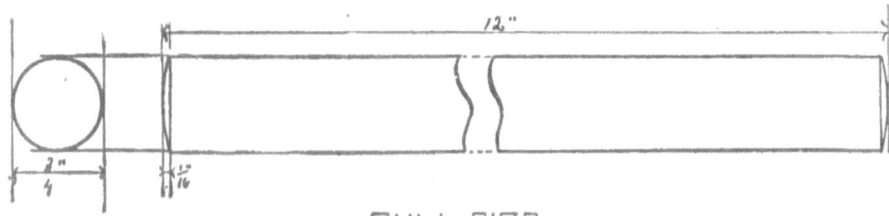

FULL SIZE.

Have the pupil cut from a 7-8" board a piece 1" x 13" and from this prepare an oblong 13-16" x 13-16" x 12 1-64". Quadrisect all edges of both ends and join opposite points except middle points. Plane corners to lines making an octagonal prism. Model corners with the plane making a cylinder. Round the ends with knife according to drawing and finish with file and sand-paper.

Model No. 10. - Paper Knife

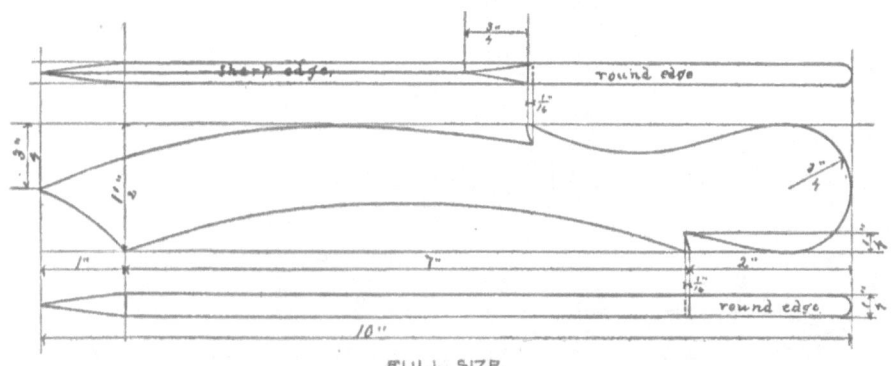

FULL SIZE.

Have the pupil cut from a 1-2" board a piece 2" x 11". With the use of axe, plane, tenon-saw and knife prepare an oblong 9-32" x 1 9-16" x 9 1-8". Place drawing upon one of the sides and with the use of tenon and turning-saws

77

cut to within 1-16" of the line. Cut with the knife and file up to lines. Round and sharpen edges according to drawing. Finish with file, scraper and sandpaper.

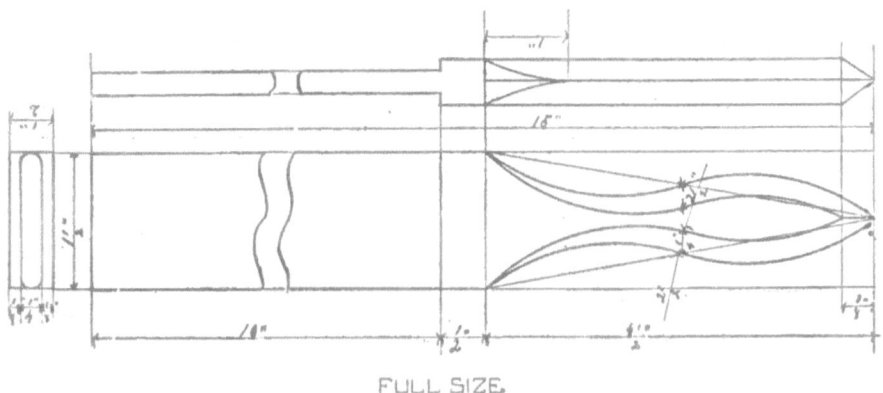

Model No. 11. – Hone

FULL SIZE.

Have the pupil cut from a 3-4" board a piece 1 3-4" x 16". Prepare from this an oblong 9-16" x 1 9-16" x 1.3 1-16". Draw plan upon two opposite sides of wood. Mark off for the 1-4" thickness with marking-gauge, and with tenon-saw cut down to these lines within 1-16" of the handle. With the use of the smoothing-plane, and chisel cut away down to the lines. Cut around the lines of handle within 1-16" of the line with the turning-saw. Round and bevel edges with knife and file according to drawing, and finish with sand-paper.

Model No. 12. - Lemon Squeezer.

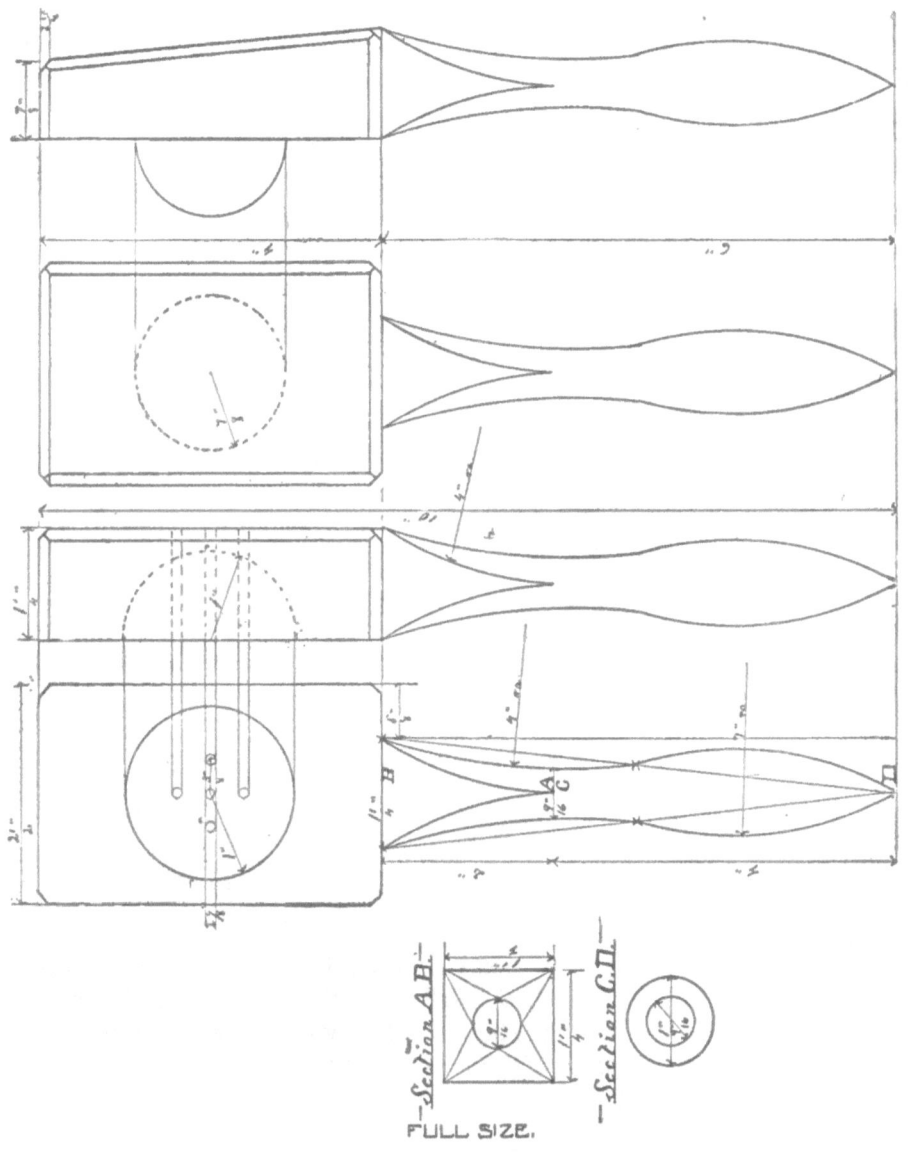

FULL SIZE.

Have the pupil cut from a 1 3-8" plank an oblong 21" x 2 3-4". Prepare from this two oblongs 1 5-16" x 2 9-16" x 10 1-8" using smoothing-plane on ends. Draw the plan upon opposite sides of wood, and with the tenon and turning-saws cut within 1-16" of the line. Cut up to line with chisel, gouge and tile. Make free hand drawing of handle upon opposite sides of the handle. Cut within 1-16" of lines with turning-saw. Cut up to lines with chisel, gouge, and tile. Model handle with knife and spoke-shave. Draw the oblique lines according to plan, and cut to lines with smoothing plane. Hollow out with gouge; bore holes with pin-bit.

Cut from a 7-8" board a piece 2" square. Draw a 1 3-4" circle upon one of the sides. Cut around circle with chisel, making a cylinder. Fasten cylinder to a piece of 1-2" board in the vice and with chisel model a hemisphere. Fasten this hemisphere in place by means of glue and a 1-4" dowel. Bevel edges with plane and knife. Finish with sand-paper and join together with a hinge.

Model No. 13. - Pen Tray

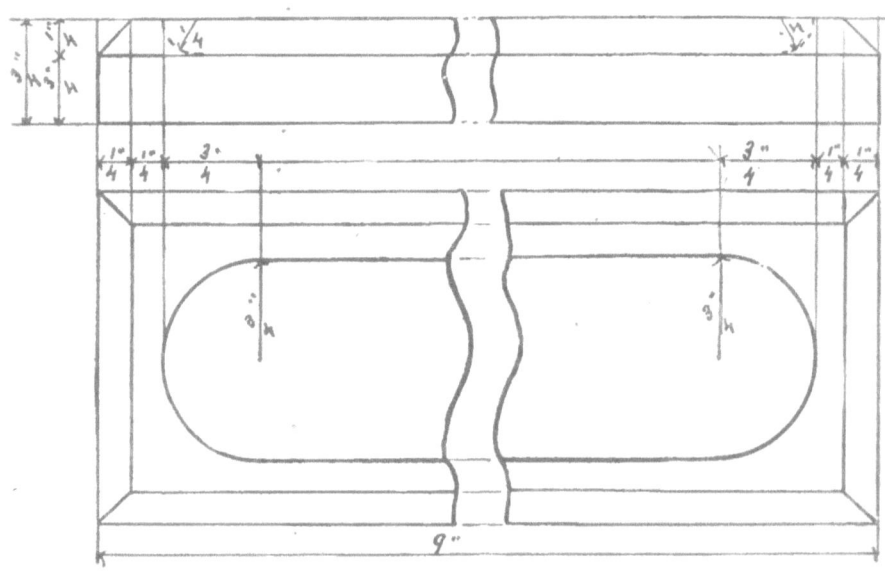

FULL SIZE.

Have the pupil cut from a 7-8" board a piece 9 1-2" x 2 3-4". Prepare from this an oblong 13-16" x 2 9-16" x 9 1-32", using block-plane on ends. Transfer plan and elevation drawing to board. Hollow with gouge. Finish bevel with plane. Finish remaining parts with sand-paper.

Model No. 14. - Cutting Board

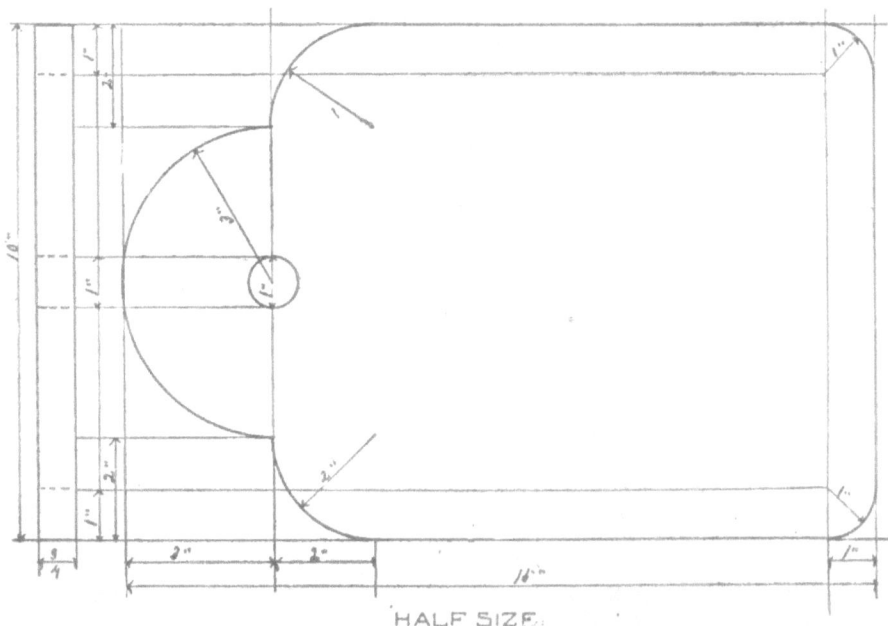

HALF SIZE.

Cut from a 7-8" board a piece 10 1-8" x 15 1-2". Prepare from this an oblong 9-16" x 10 1-16" 15 1-16". Place drawing upon the board, and bore hole with auger bit.

Cut around lines with turning-saw. Cut to lines with chisel and file.

Finish broad surface with smoothing plane; finish edges with sand-paper.

Model No. 15. - Flower Pot Rest

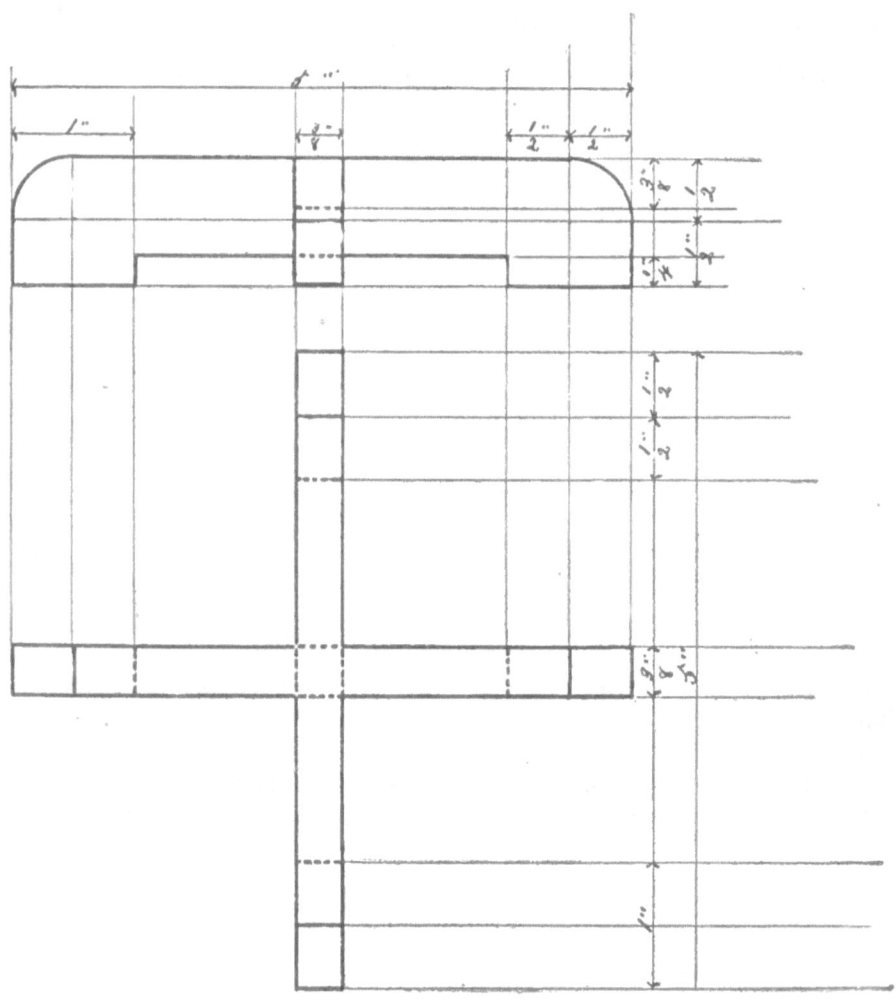

FULL SIZE

Cut from a 1-2" board a piece 1 1-4" x 11". Plane to a width of 17-32", to a thickness of 13-32". Cut this cross-wise into two equal parts. Place these two together and considering both as one, cut to an oblong 5 1-32". Draw the plan upon opposite sides. Place pieces carefully together in the vice and cut to the line with saw, chisel, knife, and file. Finish with sand-paper.

Model No. 16. - A Sugar Scoop

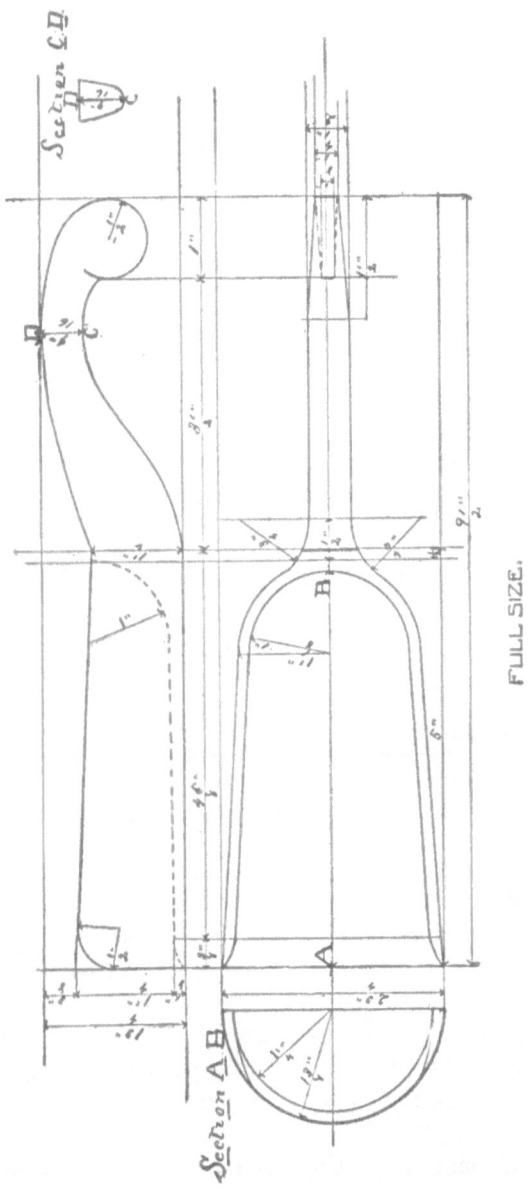

Cut from a 2" plank a piece 3" x 10". Prepare from this an oblong 1 13-16" x 2 13-16" x 9 9-16". Draw plan upon two opposite sides of wood. Cut around with splitting and turning-saw. Cut to lines with chisel, gouge, smoothing-plane and tiles. Place elevation drawing upon two opposite sides. Cut around lines, excepting handles, with splitting-saw. Cut to lines with smoothing-plane and chisel. Transfer again plan drawing. Hollow with gouge, using mallet. Cut around handle with turning saw. Model bowl with draw-knife. Cut to lines on handle with knife. Model handle with knife, and finish with rile and sand-paper.

Model No. 17. - Clothes Hanger

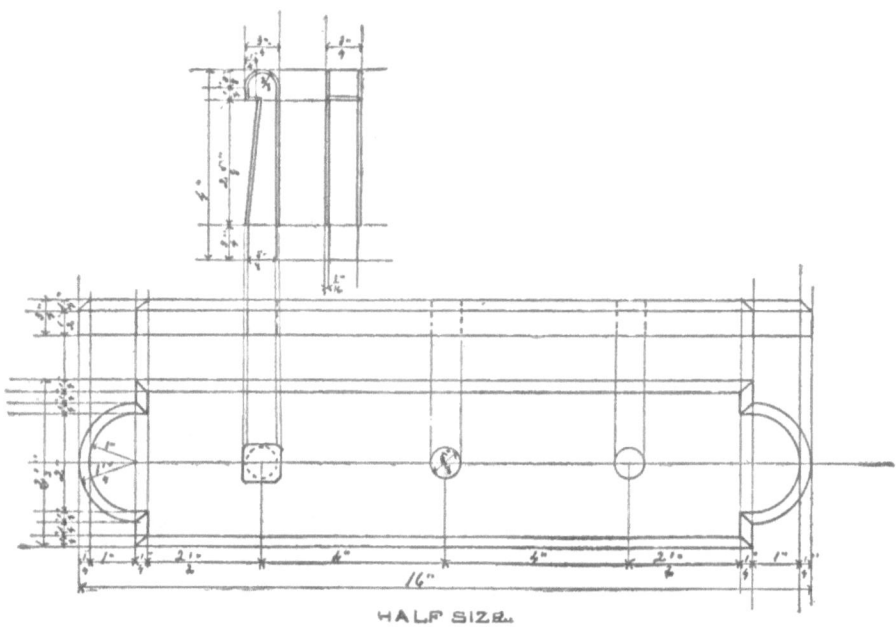

For back piece prepare from a 7-8" board an oblong 13-16" x 3 9-16" x 16 1-16". Transfer plan drawing. Bore holes with auger bit. Cut around lines with tenon and turning-saws. Cut to lines with chisel, knife and file. Bevel edges with plane, knife and file. Finish surfaces with sand-paper, except under surface.

For pins prepare from a 7-8" board a piece 1" x 13'. Prepare from this three oblongs 25-32" x 25-32" x 4 1-16". Transfer plan drawing upon opposite sides of these. Cut around lines with hacksaw; cut to lines with chisel, knife, and file.

Finish with sand-paper excepting dowels. Fasten pins to back board with glue and wedges. Finish under surface with smoothing-plane when dry.

Model No. 18. - Dish Drainer

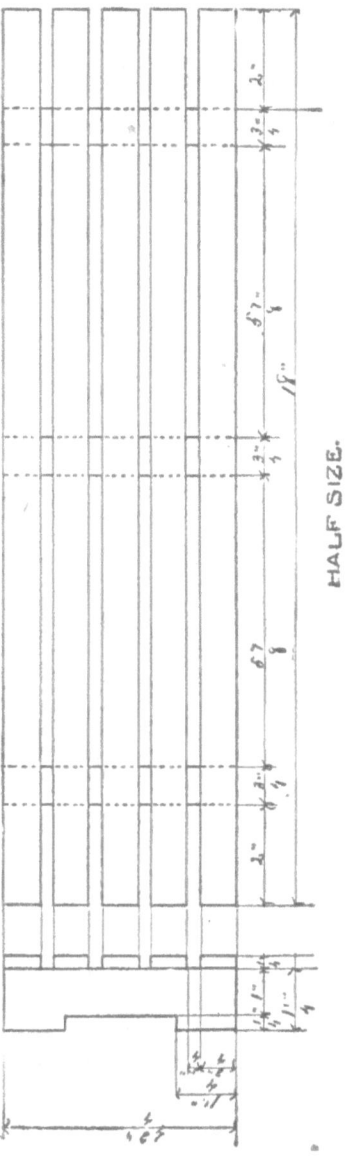

For slats prepare from a 7-8" board an oblong 25-32" x 4" x 18 1-32". With marking gauge, beginning at one of the long edges, mark off 1-4" spaces upon top and bottom surfaces. Mark first space 1, third space 2, and fifth space 3 and so on across the board. Cut between these spaces with splitting-saw. Cut to lines with jack-plane making five slats. Finish with sand-paper.

For the rests, prepare from a 7-8" board three oblongs 25-32" x 1 5-32" x 4 25-32". Draw plan upon these pieces. Cut around lines with hack-saw. Cut to lines with knife and file. Finish with sand-paper. Nail together with 1" wire brads. Sink nails with nail-set. Level up top surface with smoothing-plane and finish with sandpaper.

Model No. 19. - Towel Roller

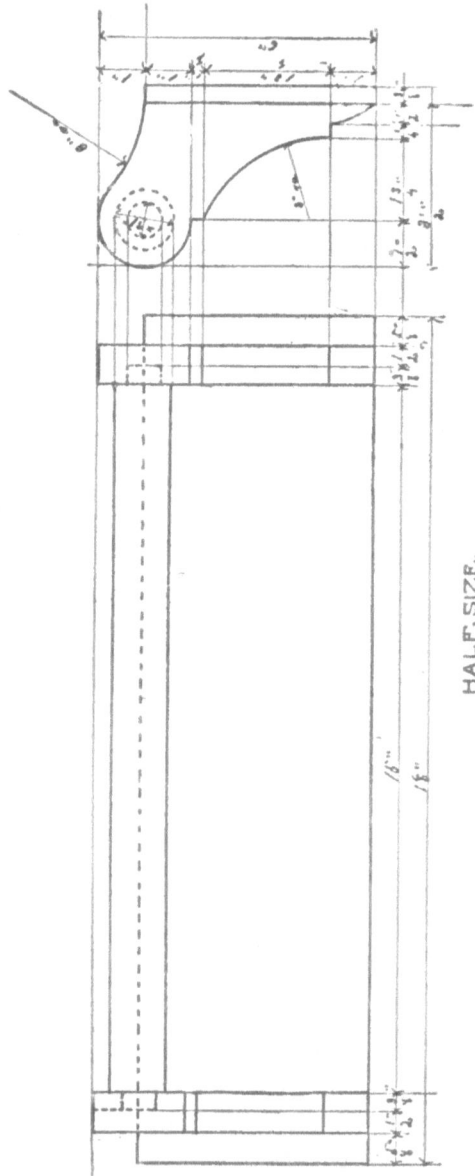

HALF. SIZE.

For roller prepare an oblong 1 5-16" x 1 5-16" x 15 3-4 . Draw diagonals on both ends. Quadrisect all edges on both ends and join opposite points excepting middle points. Plane corners to lines making an octagonal prism. Model with plane to a cylinder. Finish cylinder with tile and sand-paper. From the center of both ends draw 3-4" circle. Set off ends with marking gauge. Cut around lines with tenon-saw: cut to lines with knife and tile. Finish with sand-paper.

For back board prepare an oblong according to drawing.

For brackets prepare two oblongs 13-16 x 3 9-16" x 6 1-16". Place these together as one piece. Draw plan upon opposite sides of wood. Saw around lines with turning-saw. Cut to lines with chisel, gouge, and file. Finish edges with sand-paper.

Bore holes with auger-bit: cut slot with chisel: finish with sand-paper. Nail and screw together, using 1 1-2" brads and 3-4 screws.

Model No. 20. - Sponge Rack

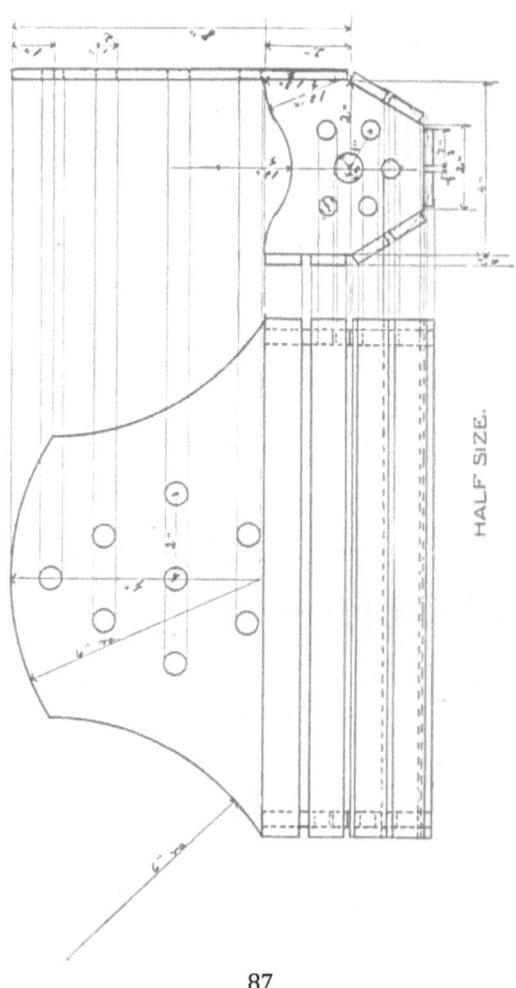

HALF SIZE.

For slats prepare an oblong 25-32" x 4" x 12 1-32" . Proceed with the making of slats as in Model No. 18.

For ends prepare two oblongs 13-32" x 4 1-32" x 4 1-32" . Place them together as one piece. Transfer plan drawing upon opposite sides, and bore holes with auger-bit: cut around lines with turning-saw; cut to lines with smoothing-plane, knife and tile; finish with sand-paper.

For back board prepare an oblong 9-32" x 8 1-16" x 12 1-32". Transfer plan drawing upon one side; bore holes with auger-bit; cut around lines with turning-saw; cut to lines with knife and tile; finish with sand-paper.

Nail together with 1" brads: set nails: level up slats with smoothing-plane; finish with sand-paper.

Model No. 21. – Blotter

Prepare for base board an oblong 5-8" x 5 1-8" x 9 1-16". Draw-plan for notch, marking over lines with knife; cut around lines with tenon-saw; cut to lines with 1-2" chisel: make a wedge 1-2' thick and 10" long to fit notch; spread glue upon wedge and in notch; drive together with mallet; finish ends of wedge with smoothing-plane; finish under surface of base board and wedge with smoothing-plane; plane base board to a thickness of 17-32"; draw plan upon opposite sides of oblong; cut to lines with chisel and file; bevel edges with chisel and file; finish with sand-paper.

For handle, prepare an oblong 13-16" x 13-16" x 5 9-16". Place hexagon upon ends; plane sides to end lines; making a hexagonal prism: set off and shape ends according to drawing: finish with sandpaper, and screw together.

Model No. 22. - Nail Box

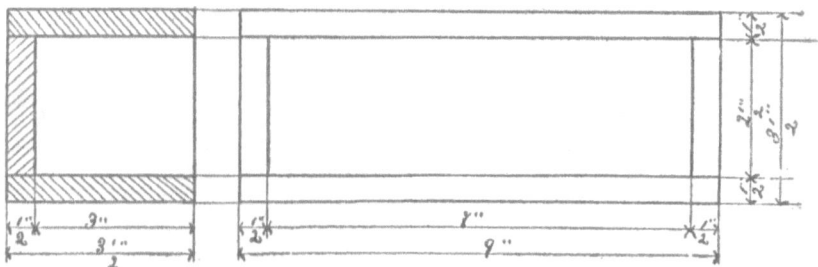

HALF SIZE.

Prepare oblongs for box according to drawing, finishing edges with a jack-plane with the help of a shooting-board; finish inside surfaces with sand-paper. Nail together with 11-4" brads; set nails and finish outside surfaces with smoothing-plane and sand-paper.

Model No. 23. - Stirring Spoon

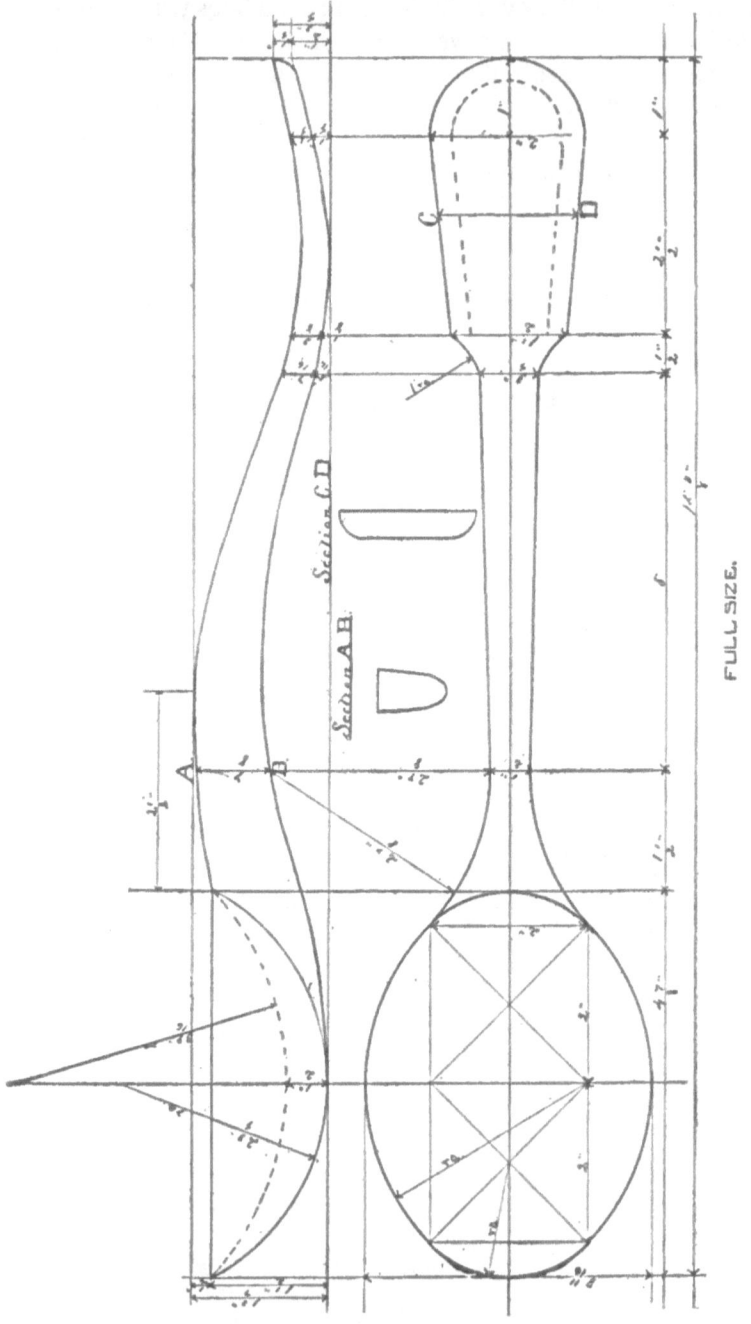

Prepare an oblong 1 7-8" x 3 3-4" x 15 1-2" . Draw plan upon opposite sides of wood; cut around lines with splitting and turning-saws; cut to lines with chisel, gouge and file: transfer elevation drawing upon opposide sides; cut around top line of bowl with splitting-saw; cut to line with smoothing-plane and chisel; hollow with gouge; finish hollowing with sand-paper; model bowl with draw-knife; cut around lines of handle with turning-saw; cut to lines with chisel, gouge and file; finish with sand-paper.

Model No. 24. - Table Mat

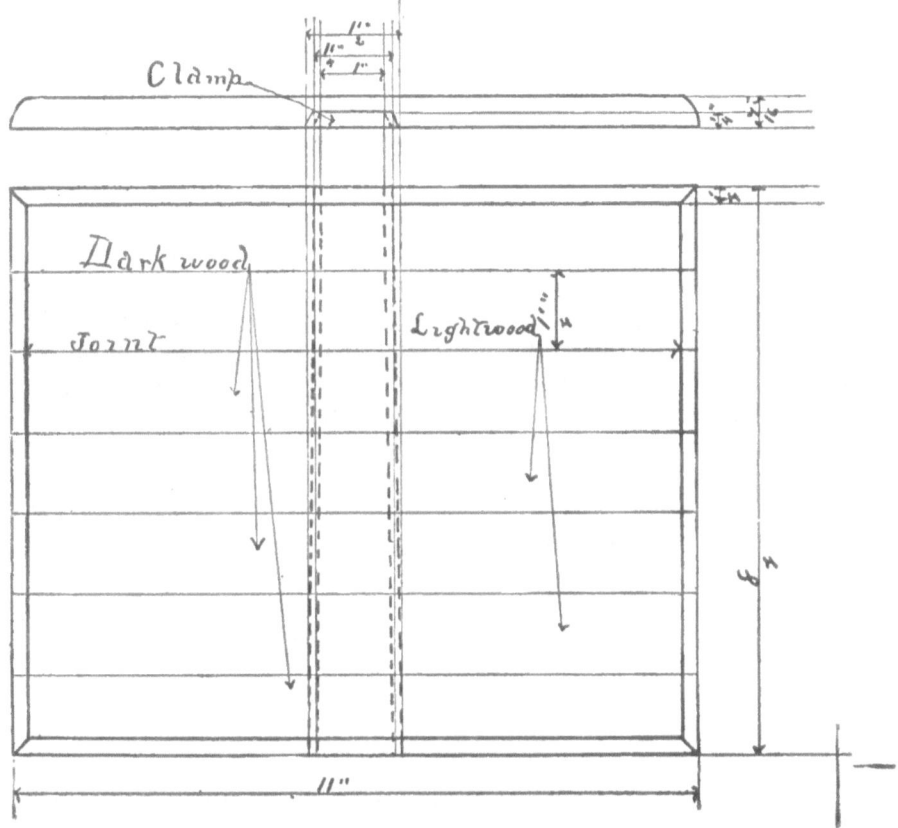

Prepare oblongs 5-6" x 1 1-4" x 12" except two side oblongs which should be made 1 3-8" in width. Glue joints; clamp in bench; make and fit wedge, and when dry plane wedge and sides as in Model No. 21.

Gauge thickness, and plane to line; bevel edges with smoothing-plane; finish with file and sand-paper.

Model No. 25. - Coat Hanger

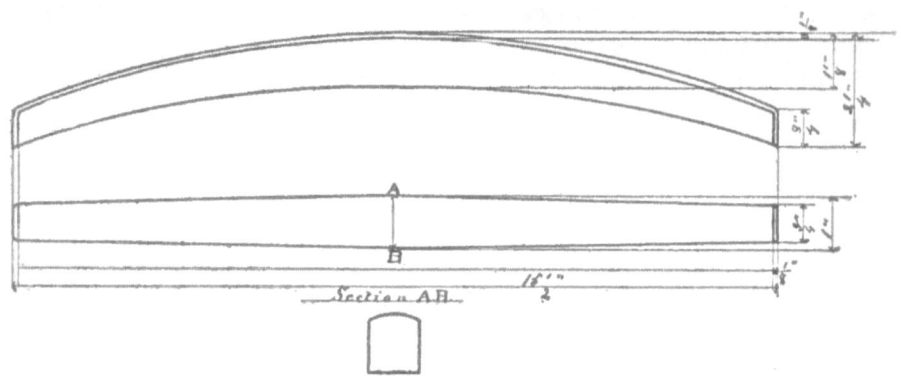

Prepare an oblong 1 1-16" x 2 5-16" x 15 17-32"; draw elevation upon two opposite sides of oblong; cut to convex lines with spoke-shave; cut to concave lines with round plane. Transfer plan drawing upon two opposite sides; cut to lines with smoothing-plane; model top surface with spoke-shave; bevel ends with knife; bore holes with auger and pin-bit; bend hook with square and round-nosed pliers; insert dowel with glue; finish with file and sand-paper.

Model No. 26. – Ruler

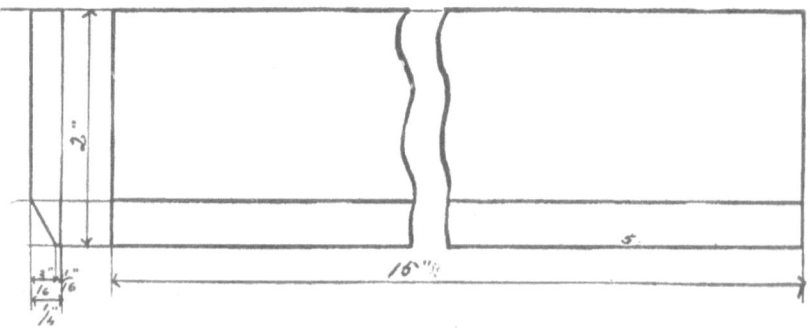

FULL SIZE

Prepare an oblong 9-32" x 2 1-32" x 15 1-32". Transfer to model, plan drawing and elevation drawing. Plane to lines; finish with sand-paper.

Model No. 27. - Bill Holder

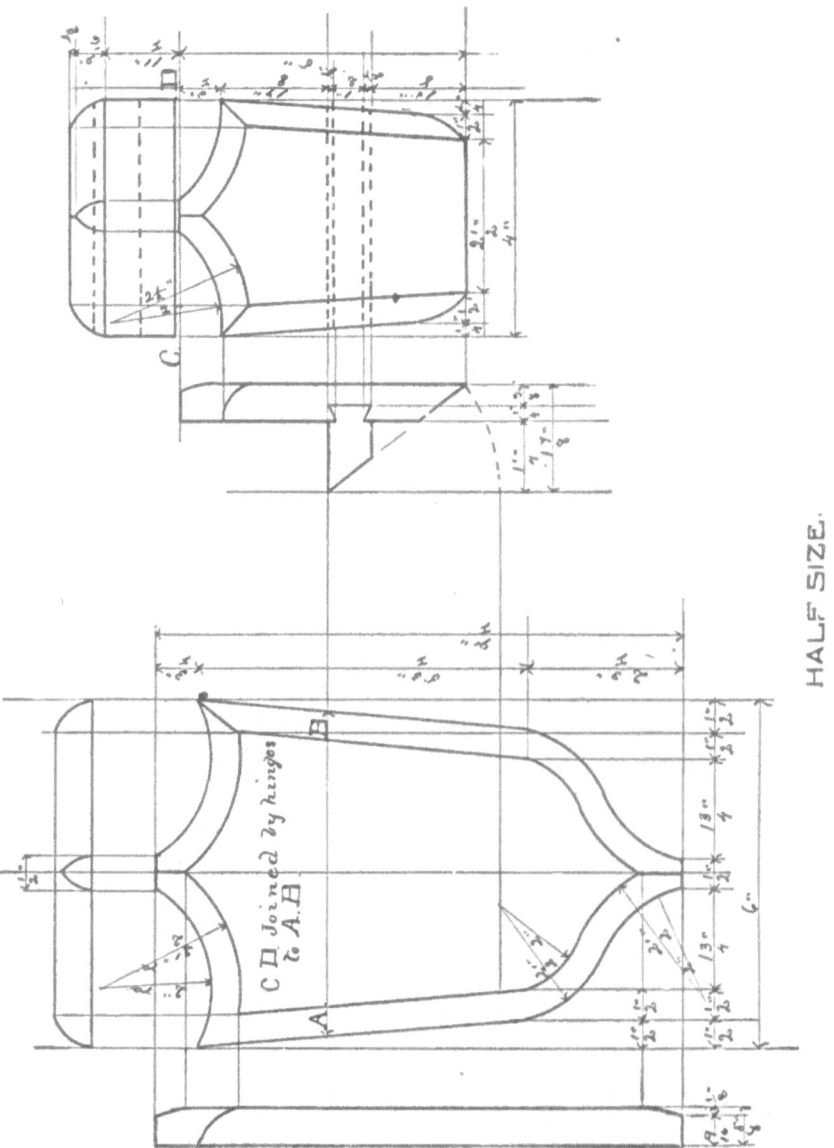

Prepare an oblong for base board 25-32" x 6 1-16" x 9 5-16". Transfer plan drawing upon opposite sides; cut around lines with splitting- and turning-saws; cut to lines with chisel and rile: bevel edges with chisel and file; finish with sand-paper.

Prepare a piece for top board 25-32" x 4 1-16 x 5 1-16"; prepare notch as in Model No. 24; prepare for middle rest a piece 25-32" x 1 9-16" x5"; pre-pare this piece for notch; glue together. Transfer drawing on top board; cut

93

around lines with turning saw; cut to lines with chisel, block-plane and file. Transfer elevation drawing to both; cut to lines with block plane; finish with sandpaper; join this to base board with hinges; insert dowels for springs.

To make spring, wind three feet of 1-16" brass wire around a 3-8" iron rod. Place spring over dowels.

Model. No. 28. - Book Rack

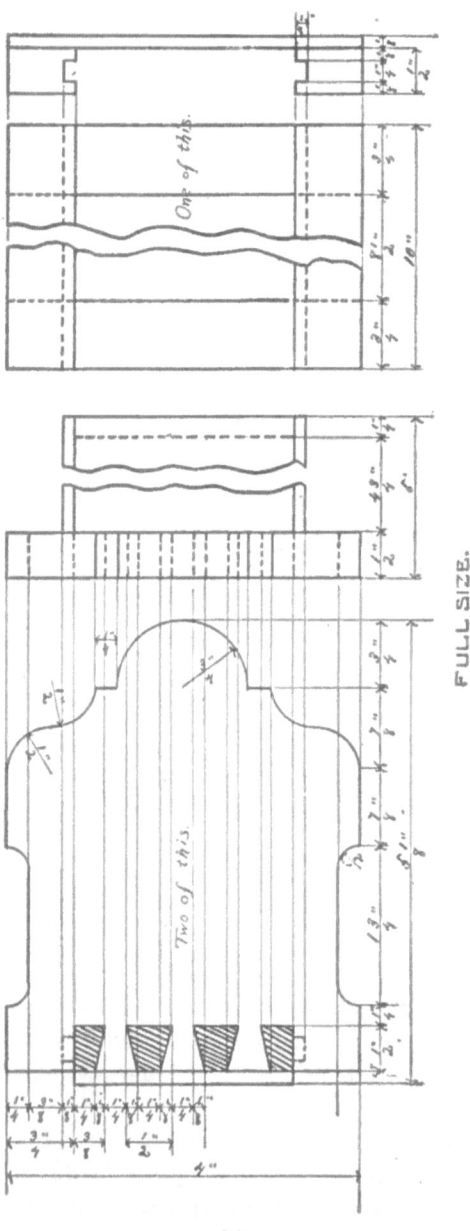

For end pieces prepare two oblongs 9-16" x 4 1-16" x 5 1-16". For pieces that are dove-tailed to end pieces prepare oblongs 9-16" x 2 3-4" x 5 1-16". Set off tongue for groove with marking-gauge; cut to lines with chisel.

Transfer drawing for dove-tail, marking over lines with point of knife, using the bevel-gauge. Cut around lines with tenon-saw: finish with chisel and knife.

Transfer drawing upon end pieces, cut around lines with turning-saw, cut to lines with chisel, gauge, and tile: cut to lines of dove-tail with knife, using bevel-gauge; cut around lines with tenon-saw; cut to lines with chisel and knife and fit to other pieces; glue joints, using mallet for driving together.

Finish with smoothing-plane and sand-paper. Prepare pieces for runs according to drawing; set off grooves with marking gauge: cut to lines with 1-8" chisel.

Prepare cross-pieces according to drawing; finish with sandpaper; glue and nail together, using 3-8" brads.

Model No. 29. - Mail Box

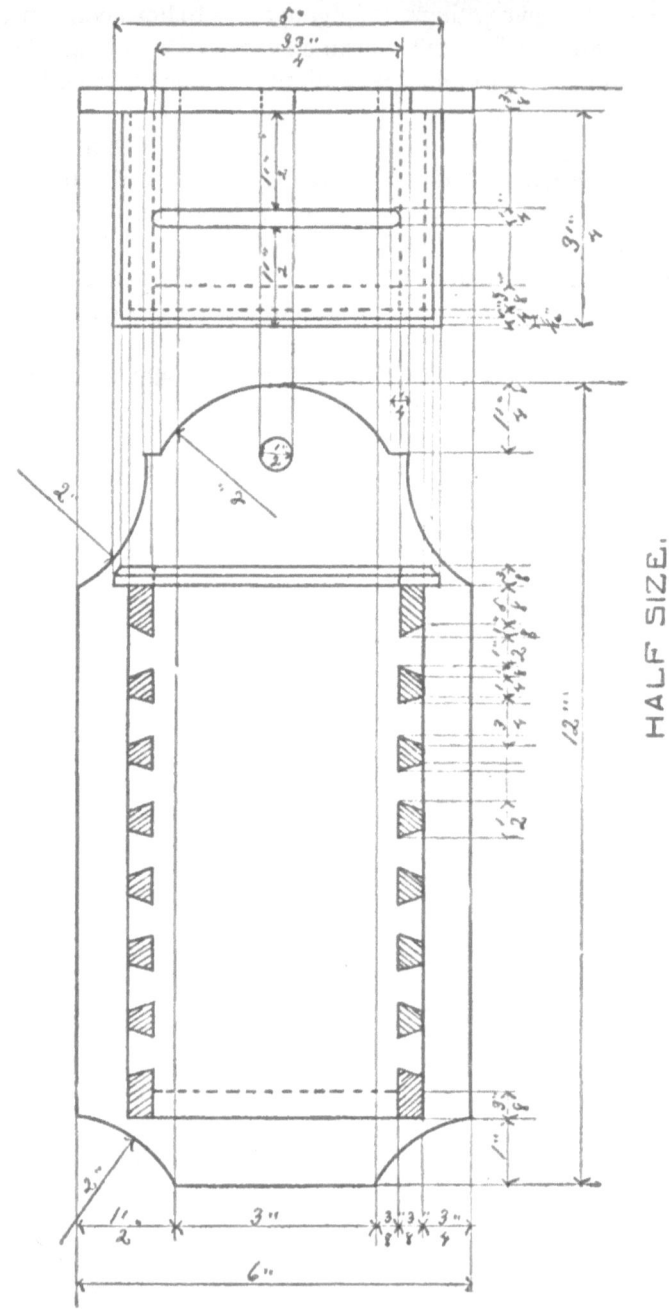

HALF SIZE.

Prepare back board according to drawing. Prepare oblongs for sides and front piece, allowing 1-16" in all dimensions.

Prepare dove-tailed joints as in model No. 28. Glue together dove-tailed joints. Finish inside faces with sand-paper. Finish outside faces with smoothing-plane and sand-paper.

Prepare bottom piece and insert it with brads and glue.

Glue, nail and clamp all to back board.

Prepare cover, making opening with auger bit, chisel, and file; join cover with hinges to back board.

Finish with sand-paper.

Model No. 30. - Pulley Block

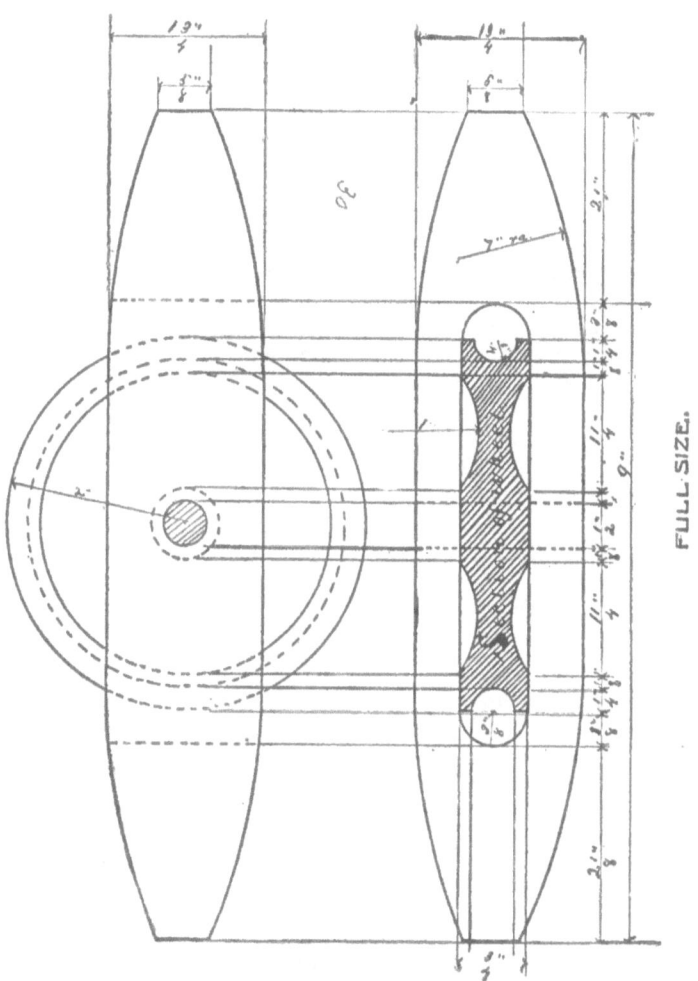

Prepare oblong for block; make opening with auger bit, chisel, and rile, working from both sides; curve ends, according to drawing, with spokeshave and file. Finish with sand-paper.

Prepare cylinder for wheel according to drawing; bore hole for spindle; hollow with gouge and rat-tail file; finish with sand-paper.

Prepare spindle, insert it in block and wheel, placing glue upon that part which extends through the wheel.

Finish ends of spindle with knife and sand-paper.

Model No. 31. - Knife Box

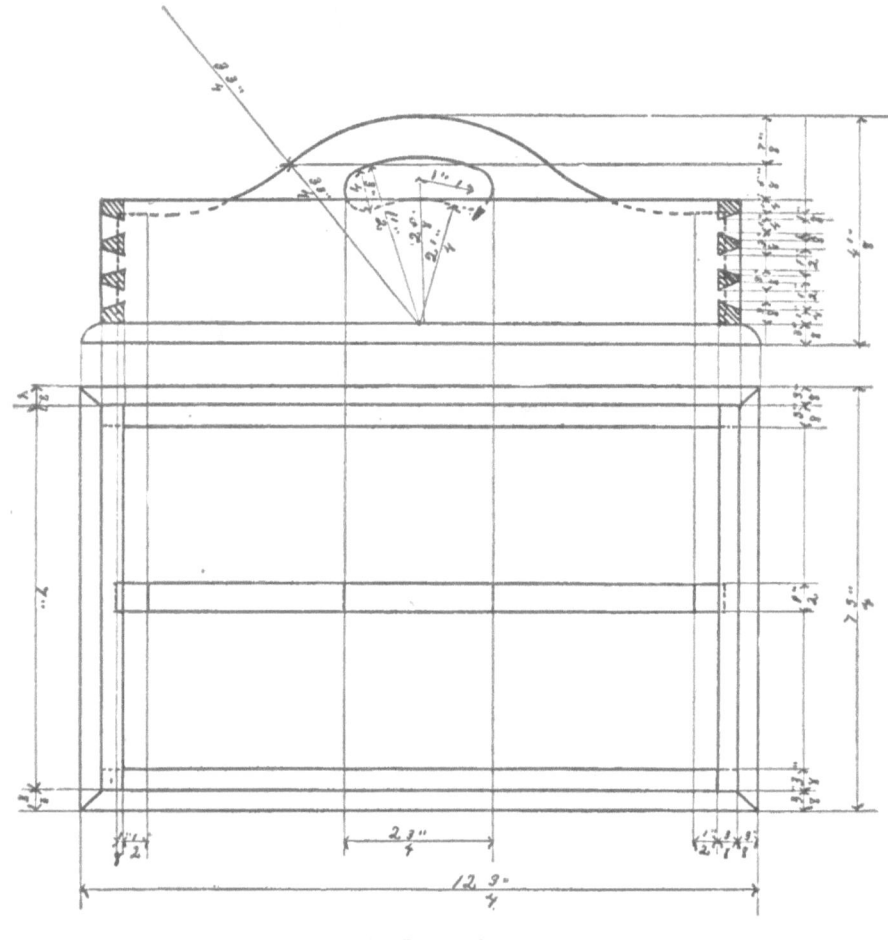

HALF SIZE.

Prepare sides and end pieces; prepare end pieces for housing; finish inside surfaces with sand-paper; dove-tail and glue together; finish outside surfaces with smoothing-plane and sand-paper.

Prepare middle piece and insert it with glue into end pieces.

Make bottom piece and fasten it with glue and brads to sides and ends. Finish with sand-paper.

Model No. 32. - Axe Handle

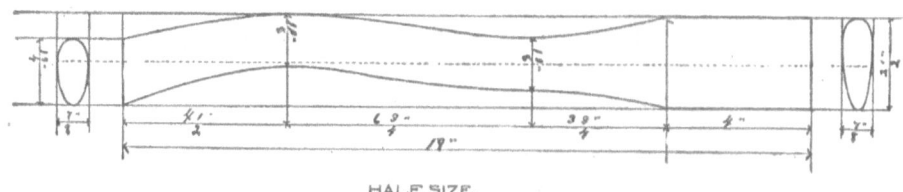

HALF SIZE.

Prepare an oblong. Transfer drawing on opposite sides; transfer drawing upon ends; cut around lines with turning-saw; bevel edges with draw-knife; model with spoke-shave, tile, and scraper. Finish with sand-paper.

Model No. 33. - Copper Stick

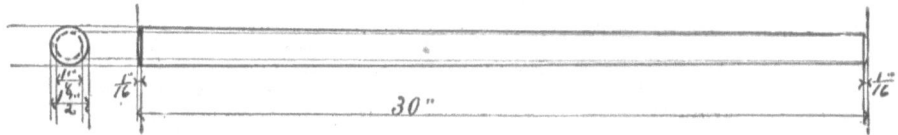

Prepare oblong and proceed as in model No. 1. Cut to lines with jack-plane. Finish with file and sand-paper.

Model No. 34. - Set Square

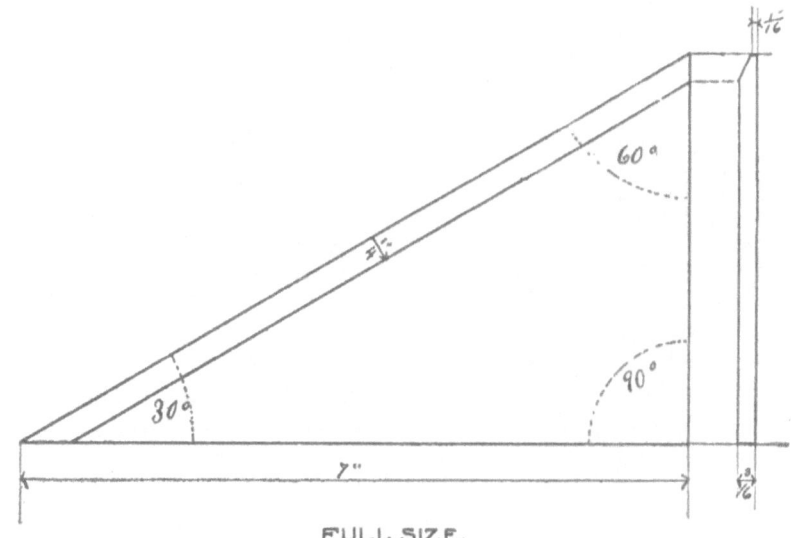

FULL SIZE.

Prepare oblong; bore hole with auger-bit; transfer plan drawing; cut to lines with smoothing-plane.

Transfer elevation drawing; bevel edge with smoothing-plane; finish with sand-paper.

Model No. 35. - Photograph Frame

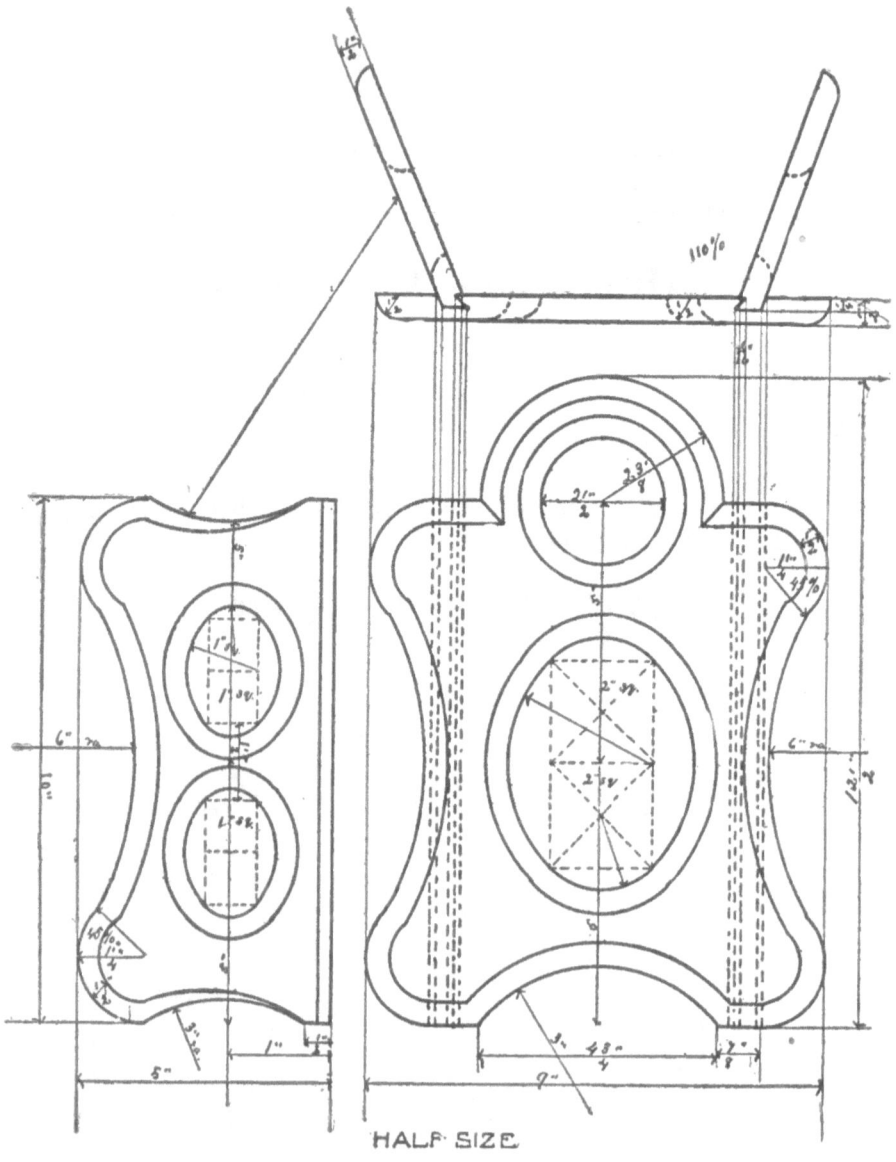

HALF SIZE

Prepare oblongs for front and sides; transfer drawings: cut around outside with turning-saw: cut around openings with key-hole saw; cut to lines with chisel, gouge and file. Finish with sandpaper.

Prepare grooving according to drawing; glue together: finish ends of glued joints with knife and sand paper.

Model No. 36. - Try-Square

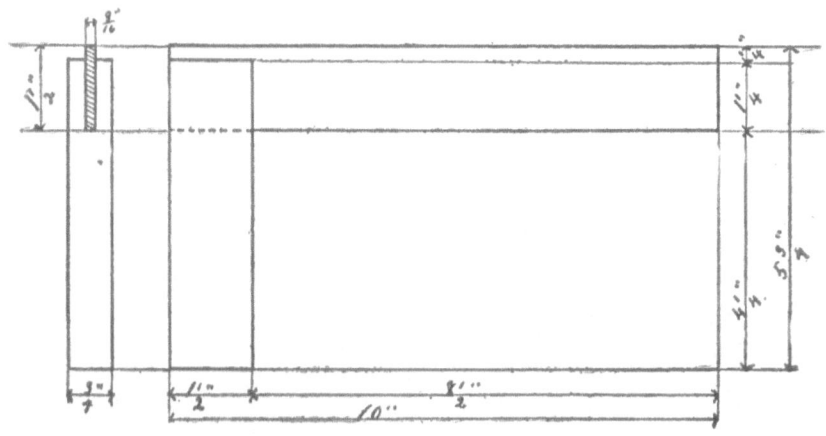

HALF SIZE.

Prepare oblongs according to drawings; set off slotting with marking-gauge; cut around lines with tenon-saw; cut to lines with 1-8" and 1-2" chisel. Glue together using clamp; bore hole with auger-bit. Finish with sand-paper.

Model No. 37. - Silver Box

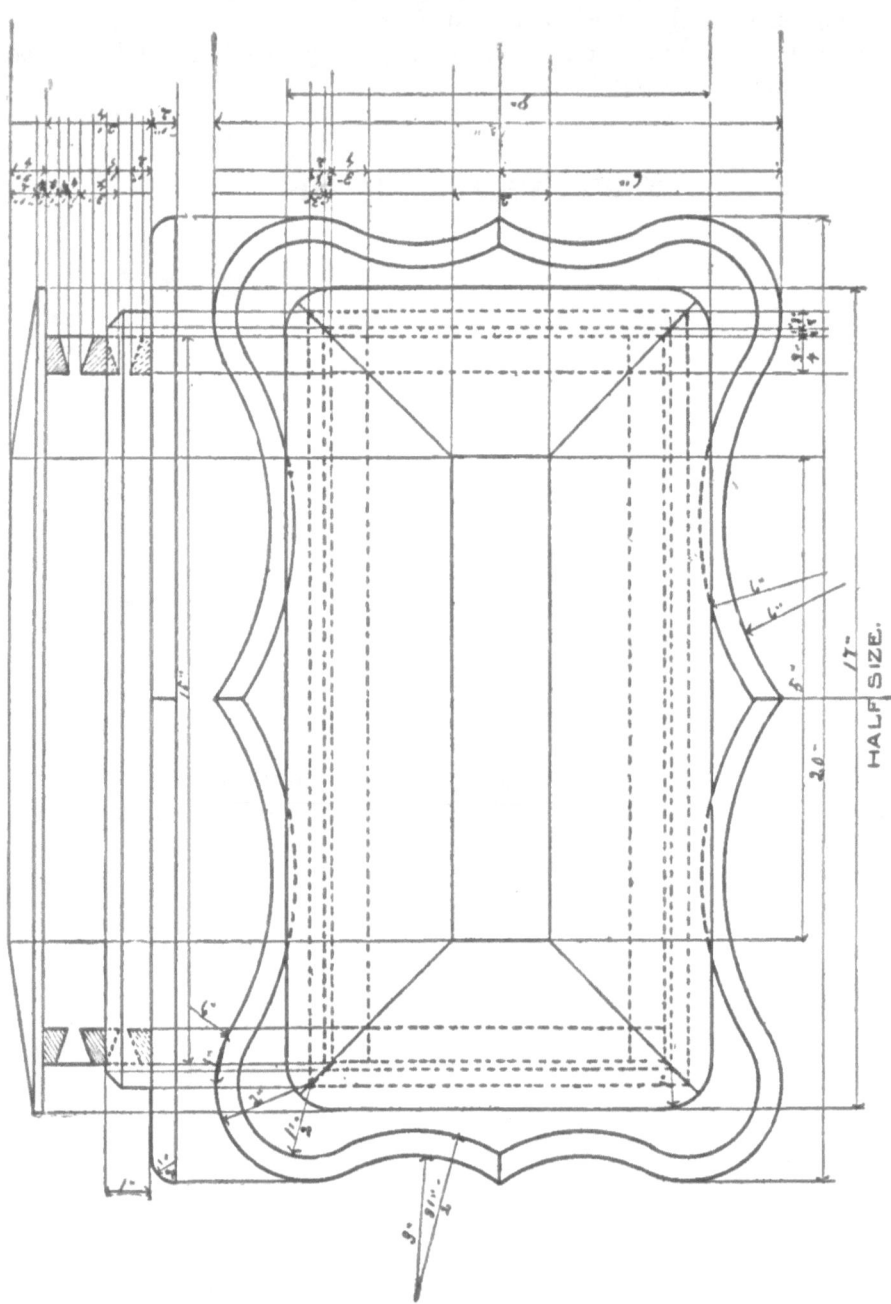

Prepare bottom and cover according to drawing; finish with sand-paper.
Prepare sides and ends for dove-tailing: allowing 1-16" in all dimensions;

make dove-tail joints and glue together; finish sides as in No. 31; glue and nail sides to bottom piece.

Prepare pieces for mitring; cut and fit mitred-joints; nail and glue to box; finish with sand-paper.

Attach cover to box with hinges.

Model No. 38. - Marking Gauge

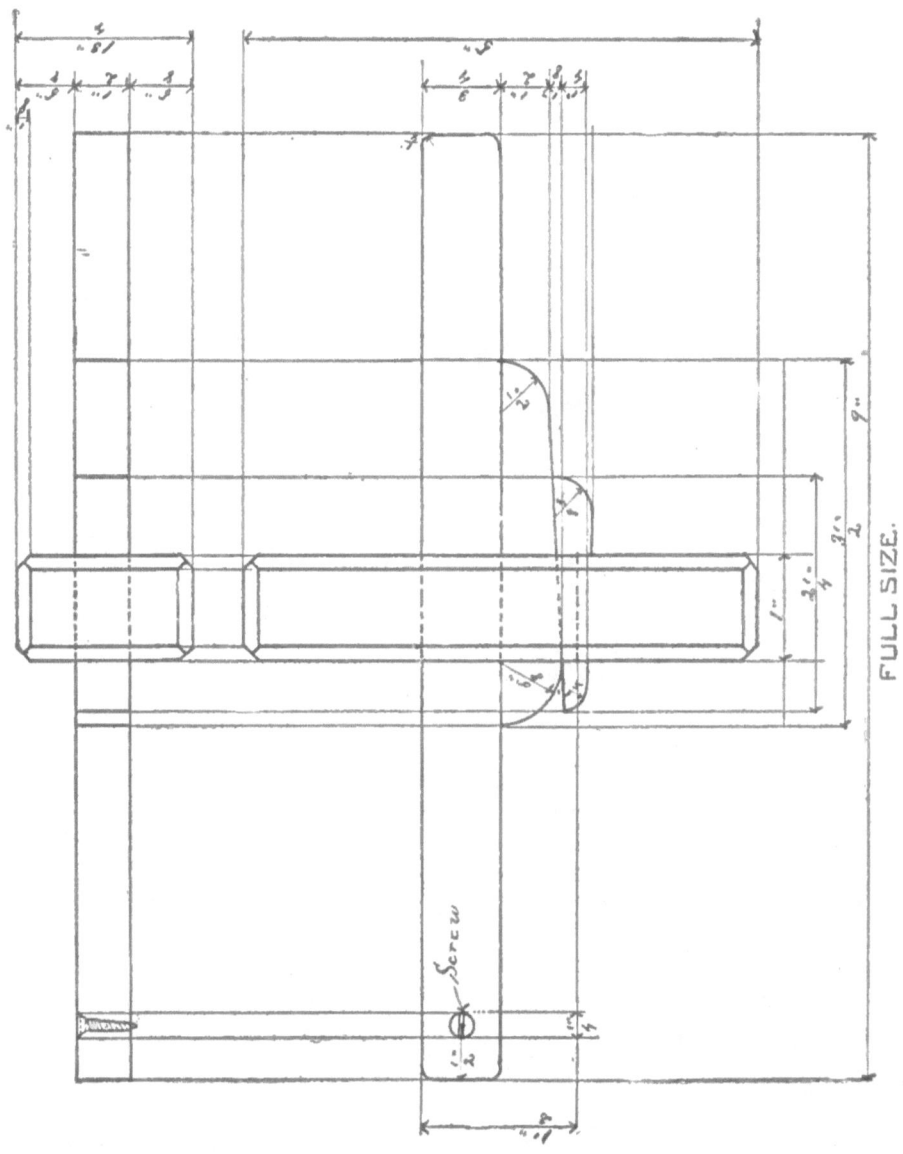

Prepare piece for mortising; set off mortice with marking-gauge; make mortice with 1-4" auger-bit and 1-4" and 1-2" chisel.

Prepare piece containing the screw and insert the screw; sharpen screw point with saw-file; make and lit keys.

Finish with sand-paper.

Model No. 39. - Wall Bracket

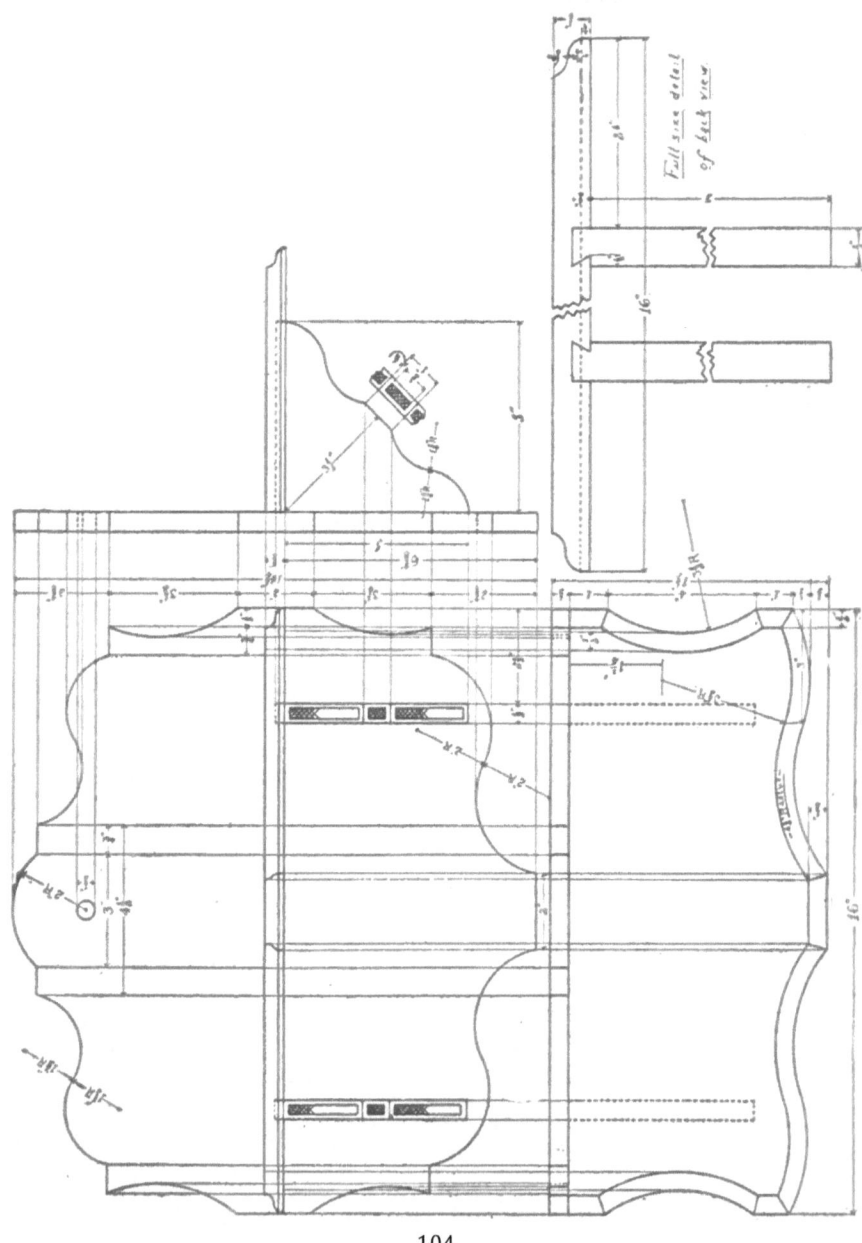

Prepare back board according to drawing. Prepare shelf and brackets, using 1-4" gouge and 1" chisel on edges of shelf and the parting-tool for graving on brackets; finish with sand-paper.

Prepare and fit notched dove-tail, inserting with glue.

Fasten shelf and bracket to back boards with screws.

Model No. 40. - Comb and Brush Case

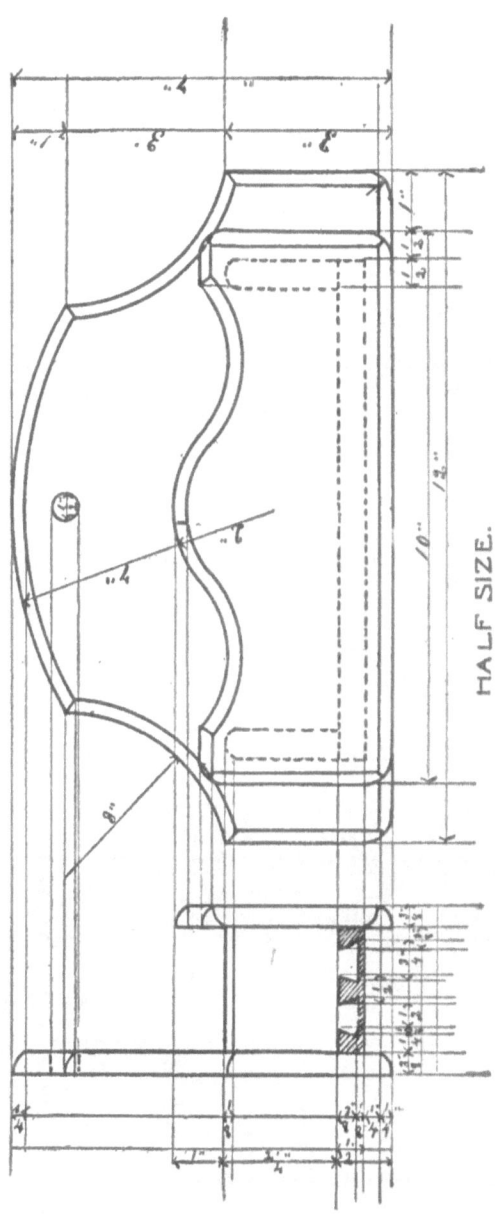

Make back and front board according to drawing-. Prepare, fit, and glue dove-tailed joints. Finish outside with smoothing-plane and sand-paper. Nail, glue and clamp to back.

Model No. 41. - Bureau Tray

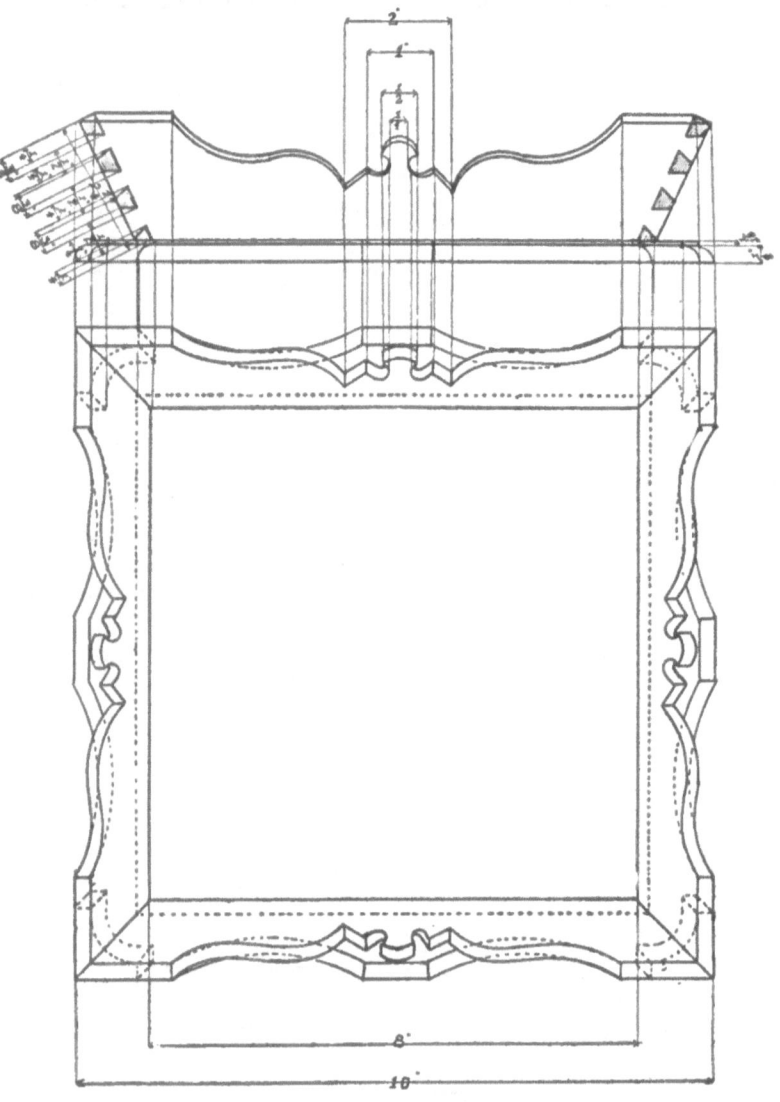

HALF SIZE.

Make bottom board according to drawing and finish with sandpaper. Prepare side pieces.

Make, glue and finish dove-tailed joints. Finish outside surfaces with block-plane and sand-paper. Glue and clamp sides to back.

Model No. 42. – Ottoman

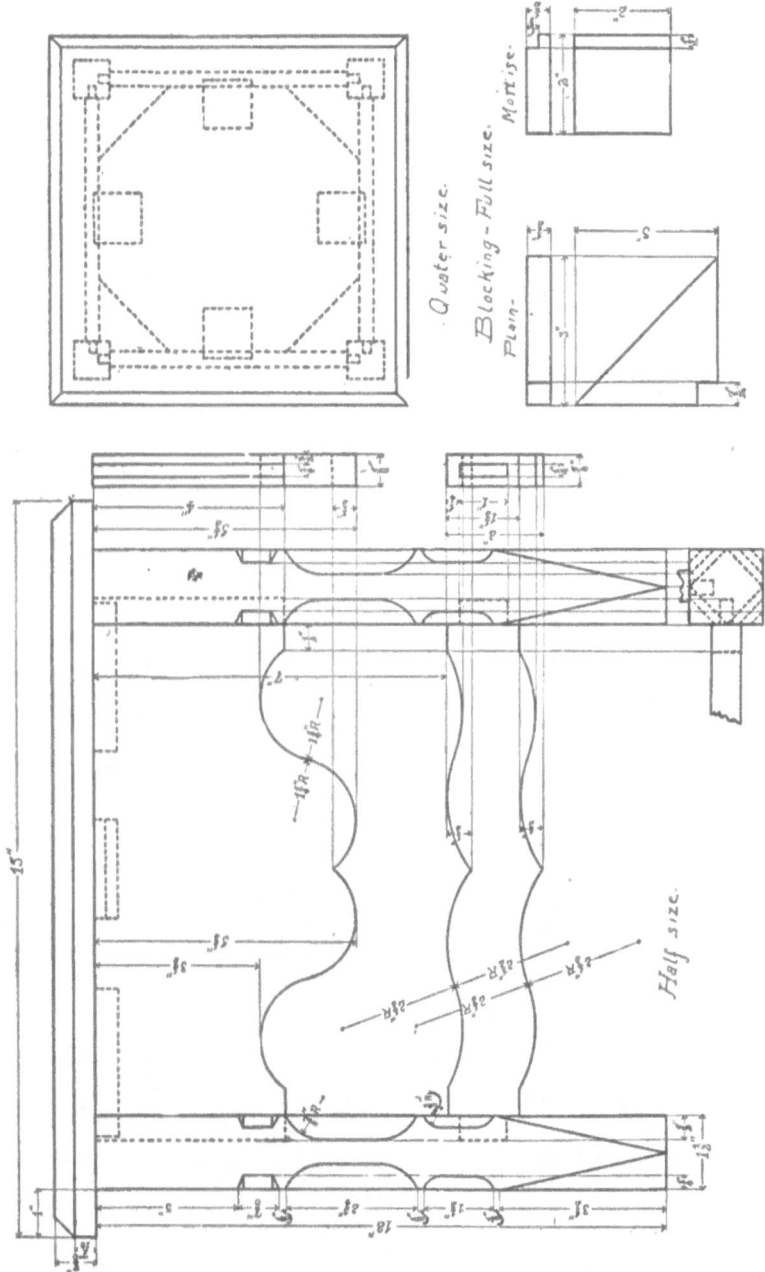

Prepare oblongs for legs. Set off mortice in legs: make mortice with 1-4"
auger-bit and 1-4" and 1" chisel; bevel and chamfer legs.

Prepare side pieces; set off tenon with marking-gauge: make tenon with
tenon-saw and 1" chisel; make mortice in side pieces for mortice-blocking;
lit, glue and clamp together mortice and tenon-joints.

Prepare top piece; glue top piece to sides and legs with common blocking
and mortice and tenon-blocking.

Model No. 43. - Cabinet

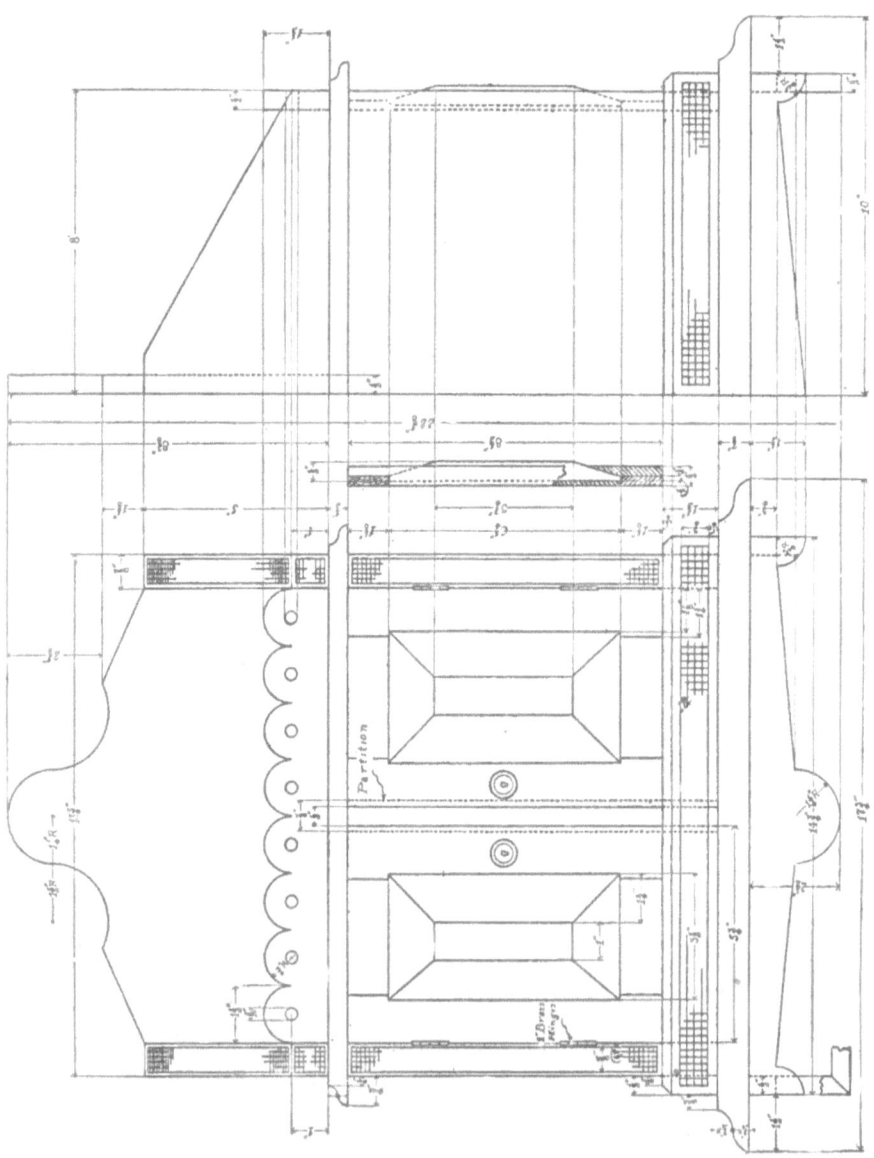

Prepare base board, side pieces, upper shelf, and partition; do graving on side pieces; glue and screw together base board, side pieces, partition and upper shelf. Make and fit back. Glue and screw back in place.

Prepare pieces for doors; make half-lap joint for doors, using marking gauge, tenon-saw and 1" chisel.

Glue and clamp together half-lap joints; finish surfaces with smoothing-plane. Do rebating with 1-4" chisel.

Make, fit, and glue panels in doors. Hang doors with hinges.

Fit locks; make and fit ornamental pieces above and below; glue and nail them in place. Finish with sand-paper.

Analysis of Models. Series Four

No.	Name.	Wood.	New Tools.	New Exercises.
1	Glove-mender.	White pine.	Knife.	Long cut, Cross cut.
2	Seed-planter.	Whitewood.	Plane.	Edge planing, Oblique cut.
3	Round flower-stick.	Pine.	Crosscut-saw.	Sawing off.
4	Letter-opener.	Cherry.	Marking gauge, Tenon-saw.	Gauging.
5	Square flower-stick.	Pine.	Splitting-saw.	Long sawing.
6	File handle.	Whitewood.	File, Pin-bit.	Filing, boring with pin-bit.
7	Key-label.	Whitewood.	Auger-bit.	Boring with auger-bit.
8	String winder.	Whitewood.	Turning-saw, Half-round file.	Convex sawing.
9	Round-ruler.	Pine.		Bevelling, convex modelling with plane.
10	Paper knife.	Cherry.	Axe, Scraper.	Chopping, broad surface cut, scraping.
11	Hone.	Cherry.	Chisel.	Stop-planing, paring.
12	Lemon-squeezer.	Whitewood.	Gouge, Spoke-shave.	Gouging, modelling with spoke-shave, end planing, oblique planing.
13	Pen-tray.	Cherry.	Block-plane.	Finishing with shooting plane, bevelling edge with plane.
14	Cutting-board.	Pine.		Long edge planing.
15	Flower-pot rest.	Whitewood.		Halving.
16	Sugar-scoop.	Whitewood.		Oblique sawing.
17	Clothes-hanger.	Whitewood.		Doweling, wedging.
18	Dish-drainer.	Pine.	Hammer, Nail-set.	Nailing, Nail sinking.
19	Towel-roller.	Whitewood.	Screw-driver.	Screwing together.
20	Sponge rack.	Whitewood.		
21	Blotter.	Cherry.		Dovetail clamping, concave chiseling, oblique chiseling.
22	Nail-box.	Whitewood.	Shooting board.	Square shooting.

No.	Name.	Wood.	New Tools.	New Exercises.
23	Stirring-spoon.	Whitewood.	Drawknife.	Modelling with drawknife.
24	Table-mat.	Butternut & pine.		Jointing, Cross planing, wedge planing.
25	Coat-hanger.	Whitewood.	Round plane.	Planing with round plane.
26	Ruler.	Cherry.		Planing thin wood.
27	Bell-holder.	Cherry.		Single dovetailing.
28	Book rack.	Oak.		Common dovetailing, making tongue and groove.
29	Mail-box.	Whitewood.	Gluing Clamps.	Clamping.
30	Pulley block.	Whitewood.		Hollowing with gouge, fitting axle.
31	Knife-box.	Whitewood.		Housing.
32	Axe handle.	Oak.		Hard wood exercise, bevelling with draw-knife.
33	Copper stick.	Whitewood.		Long oblique planing.
34	Set square.	Maple.		Spacing.
35	Photograph frame.	Whitewood.	Key-hole saw.	Oblique edge grooving, key-hole sawing.
36	Try-square.	Oak.		Slotting.
37	Silver box.	Whitewood.		Mitering, dovetailing thick wood, hinging.
38	Marking gauge.	Maple.		Mortising.
39	Wall bracket.	Whitewood.	Parting tool.	Notch dovetailing, graving, edge moding.
40	Comb & brush case.	Whitewood.		Half lap dovetailing.
41	Bureau Tray.	Whitewood.		Oblique dovetailing.
42	Ottoman.	Whitewood.		Half concealed & concealed mortise & tenon, blocking, mortise blocking, chamfering.
43	Cabinet.	Whitewood.		Half lapping, rebating, panelling, lock fitting.

Series Five

The different kinds of work embodied in this series of models, - namely advanced Cabinet work, Wood-carving, Staining, Varnishing, Designing, Drawing, - and the success that has accompanied the experiment, help, in a great degree to solve the problem as to how Manual Training should be taught so as to place it on a practical and an educational basis.

A pupil at the lathe, finds the work much different from what has gone before, he not only holds and guides the tools; but the material with a mighty power behind it, is driven at a speed of three thousand revolutions a minute against him, and he sees and feels that bodily harm may result, if care is not taken in the manipulation of the tools. He soon finds that it takes courage as well as skill to be able to do good work in turning.

The Equipment

The equipment for the room is as follows: A five-horse-power electric motor or steam engine, six first-class speed lathes, twelve benches, such as were used in the preceding work; one wood carving bench extending the length of the room, and a full equipment of tools, with oils, shellac, varnishes and stains. With this equipment a class of twenty-five may be taught, if the models are so arranged as to embody the different kinds of work named above.

Model No. 1. - Tool Holder
Full Size

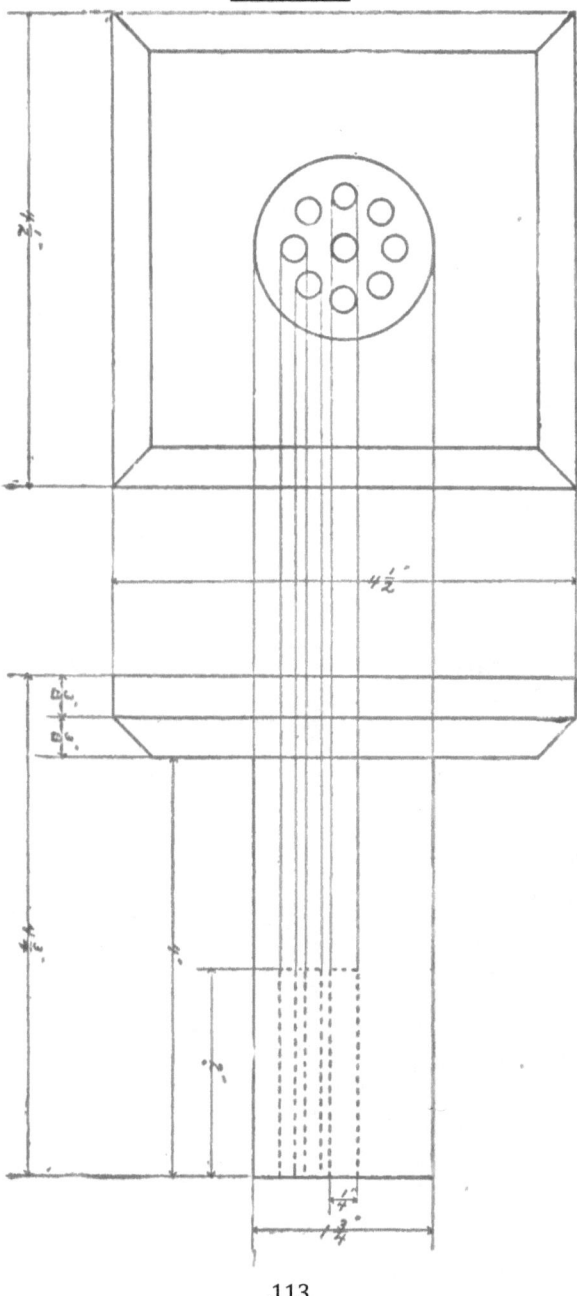

New Exercise: - Making cylinder.

Tools: - Roughing gouge, smoothing chisel, parting-tool. Wood: - White-wood, oiled and shellaced.

Note: - All staining, oiling or shellacing on turning should be done on the lathe. The roughing-gouge is used in preparing all work for the other tools, and the parting-tool is used on ends before the tool for finishing.

Model No. 2. - Gimlet Handle
Full Size

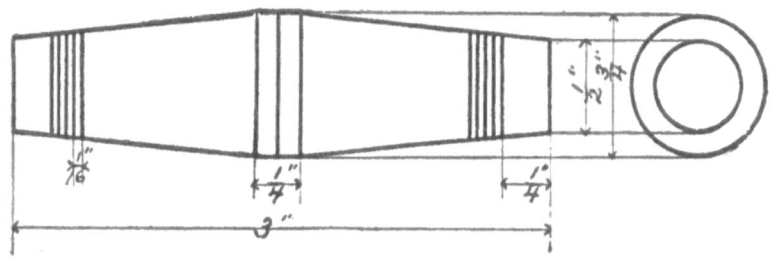

New Exercise: - Tapering.
Tool: - 1-2" Chisel.
Wood: - Cherry, oiled and shellaced.

Model No. 3. - Tool Handle
Full Size

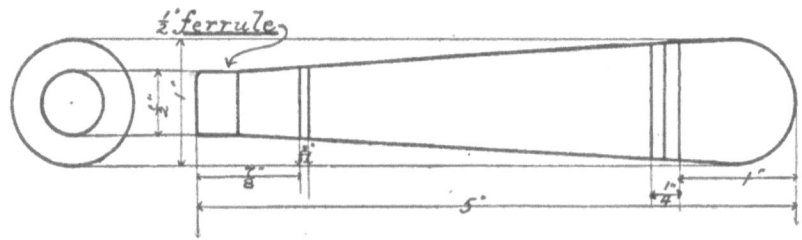

New Exercise: - Rounding end and fitting ferule.
Tool: - 1-2" Chisel.
Wood: - Maple, oiled and shellaced.

Model No. 4. - Bric-A-Brac Stand
Quarter Size

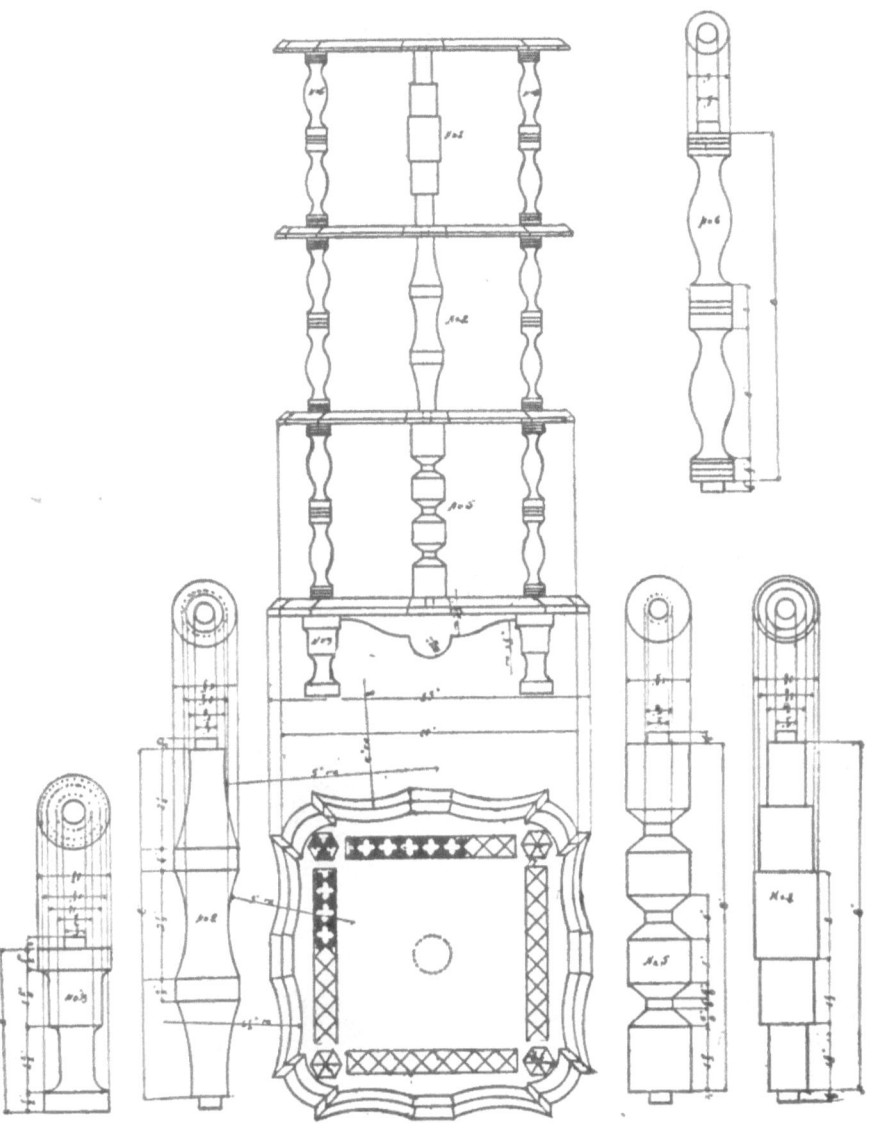

Piece No. 1. *New Exercise: - Making step cylinder. Tool: -* 1-2" Chisel.
Wood: - White wood, oiled, stained black-walnut, and shellaced.
Piece No. 2. *New Exercise: -* Concave curves. *Tools: -* Gouge and chisel.
Wood: - Same as No. 1.
Piece No. 3. New Exercise: - Reverse curves. Tools: - Gouse and chisel.
Wood: - Same as No. 1.

Piece No. 4. New Exercise: - Short concave curves. Tools: - Gouge and chisel. Wood: - Same as No. 1.

Piece No. 5. New Exercise: - Cutting down to 45° Tools: - Chisel and parting-tool. Wood: - Same as No. 1.

Shelves. New Exercise: - Carving. Tool: - Skew-chisel.

Wood: - Same as No. 1. with a coat of varnish rubbed down with pummice stone and oil.

Model No. 5. - Towel Rack
<u>Half Size</u>

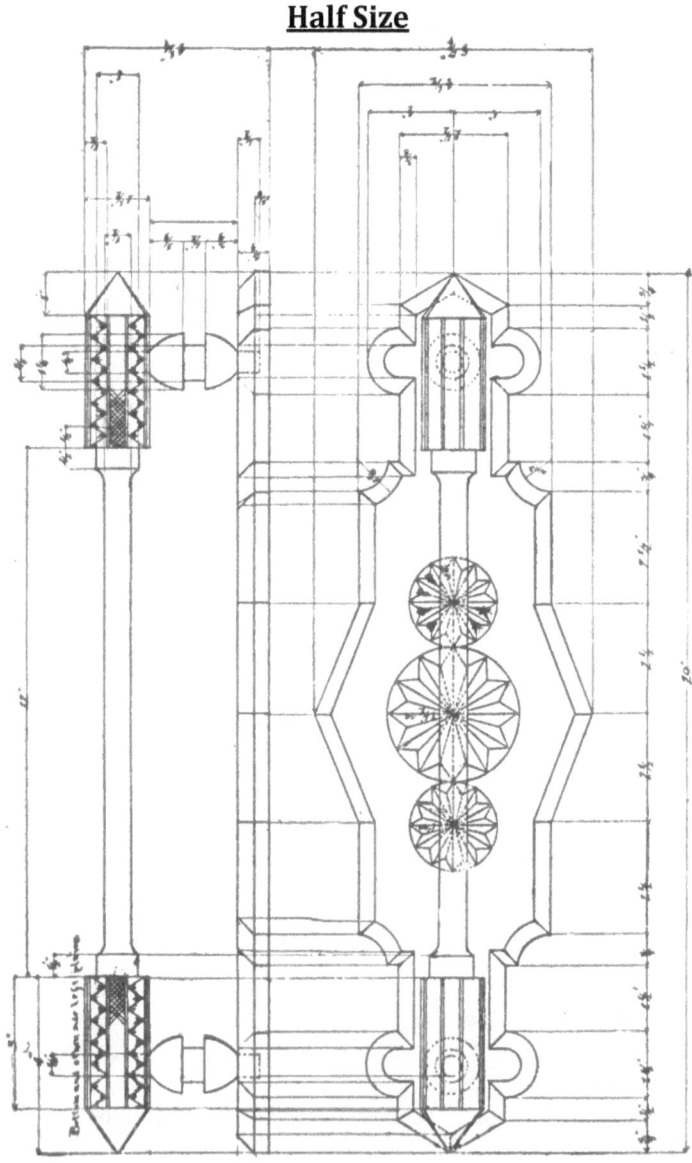

New Exercise: - Making convex, elliptical curves.
Tools: - Parting-tool, 1-2" chisel.
Tool for carving: - Skew-chisel.
Wood: - Whitewood, stained and finished as in No. 4.

Model No. 6. - Window Box
Quarter Size

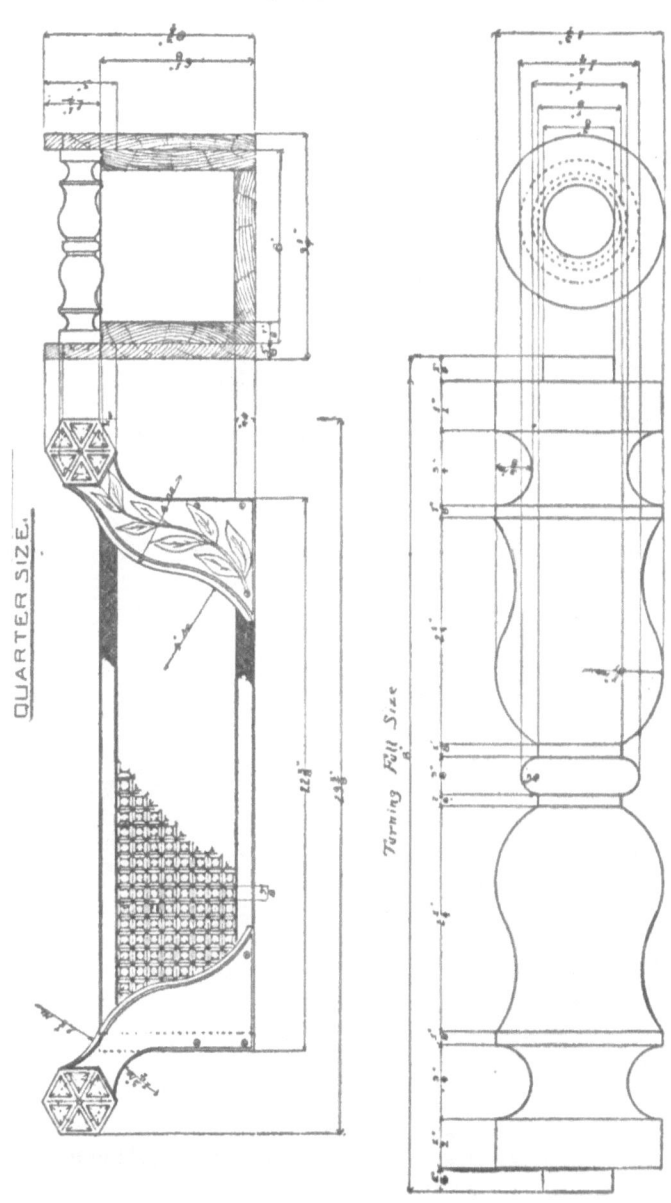

New Exercise: - Semi-circular concave curves.
Tool: - 1-2" Gouge.
Tools for cawing: - Parting-tool and skew-chisel, 3-8" gouge.
Wood: - White wood, oiled and shellaced.

Model No. 7. - Round Ruler

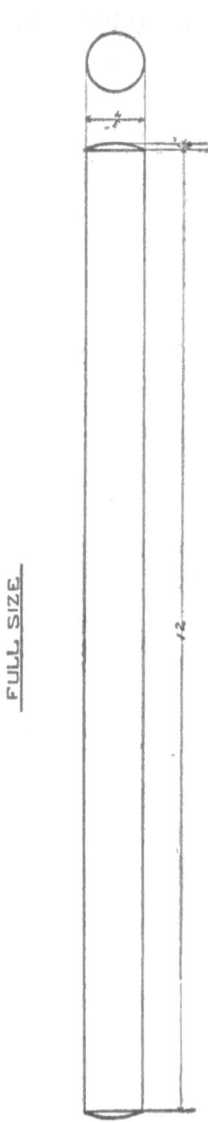

New Exercise: - Making long cylinder with convex ends.
Tools: - Smoothing-, and 1-2" chisels. *Wood:* - Cherry, oiled and shellaced.

Model No. 8. - Drawing Board Rest

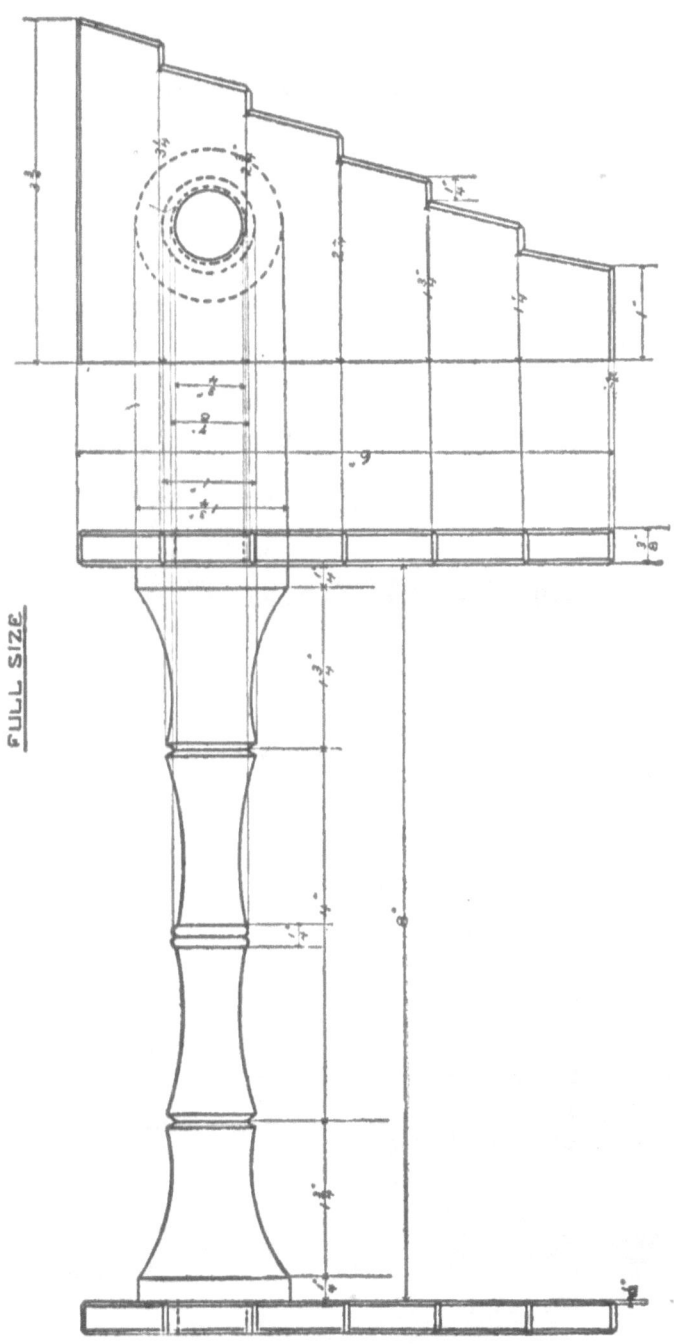

New Exercise: - Convex semi-circles.

Tool: - 1-4" Chisel.
Wood: - Whitewood, oiled and shellaced.

Model No. 9. - Key-Hanger

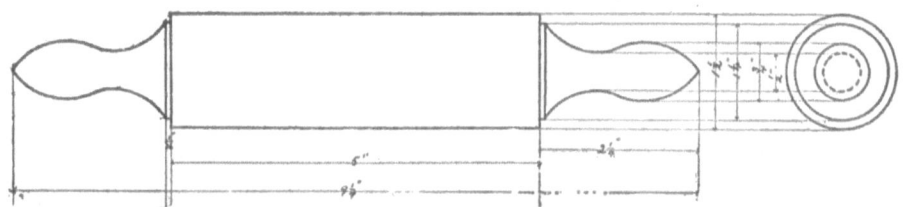

New Exercise: - Curving ends to point.
Tools: - Gouge, 1-2" chisel. Wood: - Oak, oiled and shellaced.

Model No. 10. - Stocking Mender

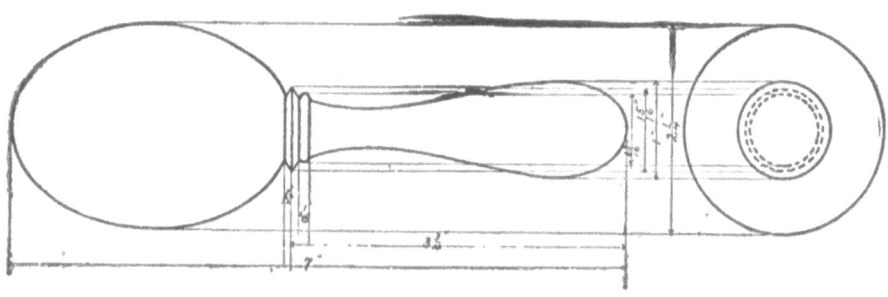

New Exercise: - Making large elliptical curves.
Tool: - 1-2" Chisel.
Wood: - Maple, oiled and shellaced.

Model No. 11. Indian Clubs

HALF SIZE

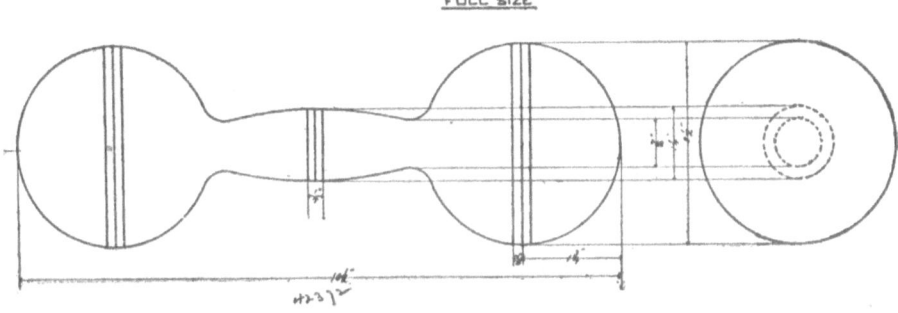

New Exercise: - Making long reverse curves.
Tool: - 1-2" Chisel.
Wood: - Whitewood, stained and finished as in No. 4.

Model No. 12. - Dumb Bells

FULL SIZE

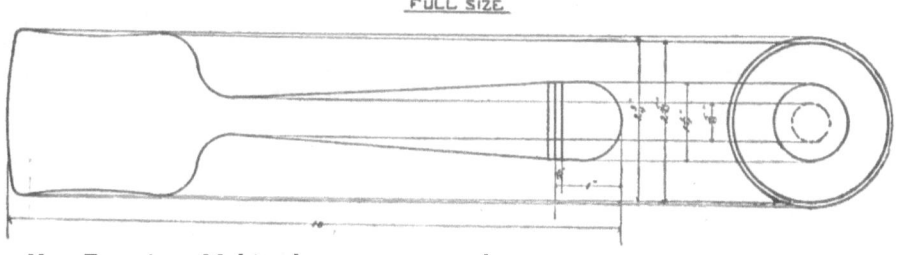

New Exercise: - Making spherical end.
Tools: - Gouge, 1-2" chisel.
Wood: - White wood, oiled and shellaced.

Model No. 13. - Potato Masher

FULL SIZE

New Exercise: - Making large convex ends.
Tool: - 1-2" Chisel.
Wood: - Maple.

Model No. 14. Mallet

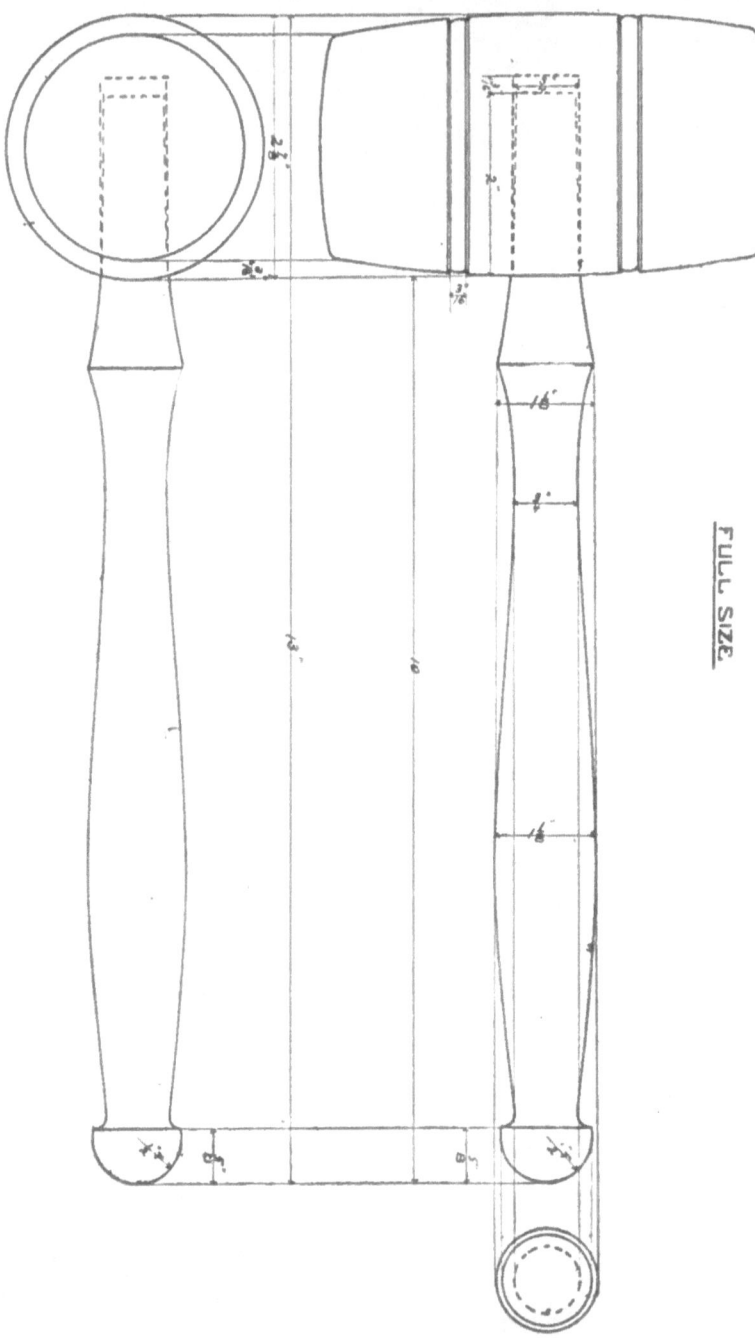

No New Exercise. Wood: - Maple, oiled and shellaced.

Model No. 15. - Book Shelves

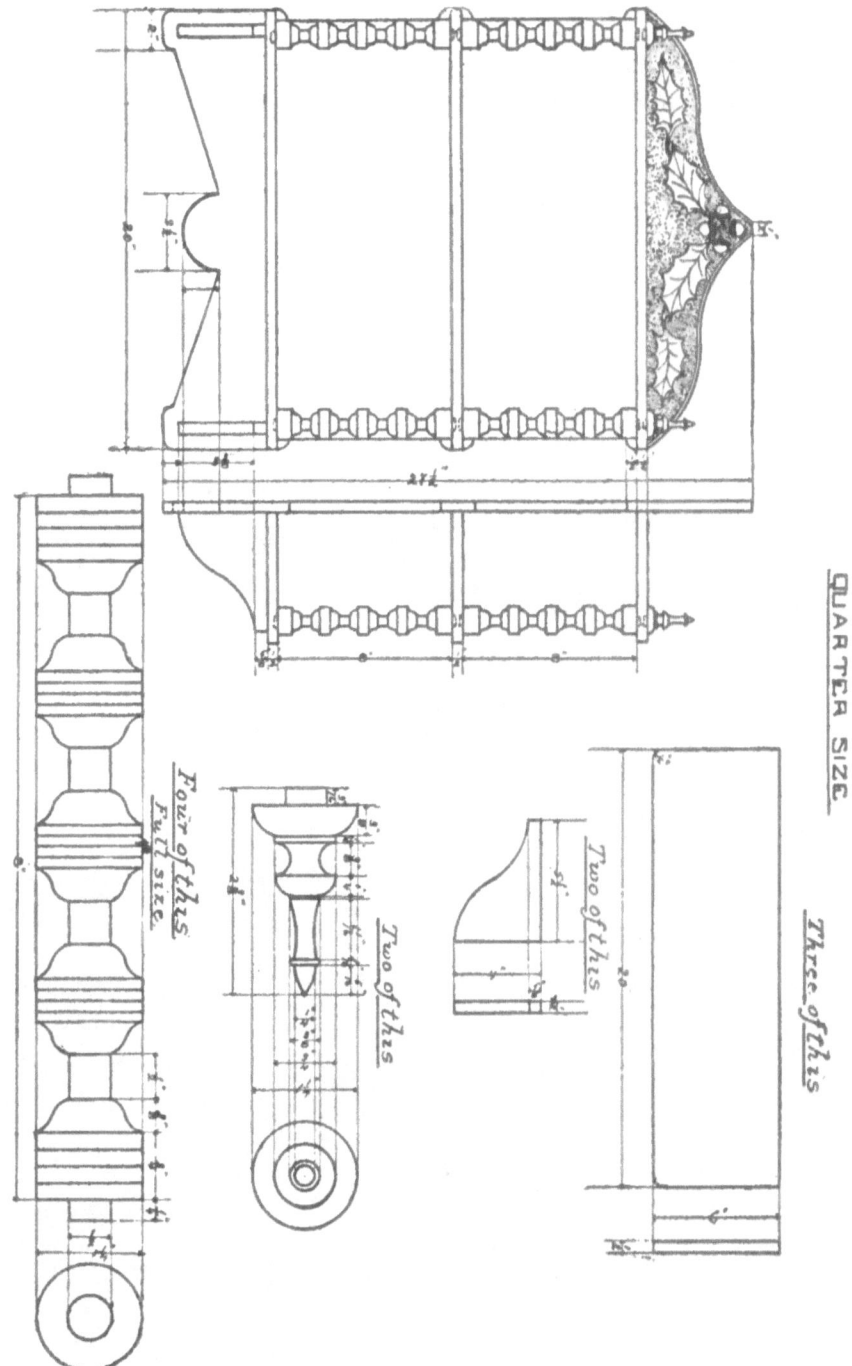

New Exercises: - Cutting down in short reverse curves.

Tool: - 1-4" Gouge.

Tools for carving: - Parting-tool, 3-8" gouge, 1-4" flat gouge, 1-2" flat gouge, 1-8" gouge, back-ground tool.

Wood: - "Whitewood, antique stained and finished as in No. 4.

Model No. 16. - Tool Handle

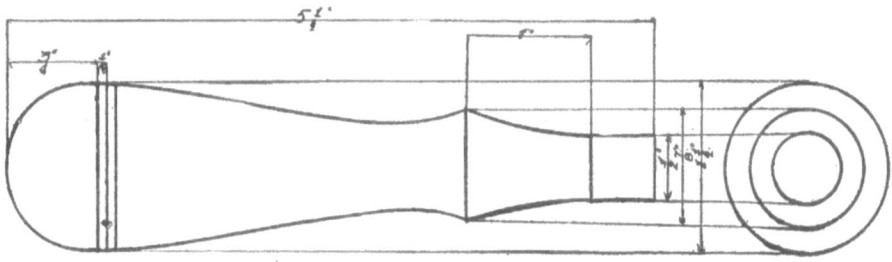

No New Exercise. Wood: - Maple.

Model No. 17. - Tool Handle

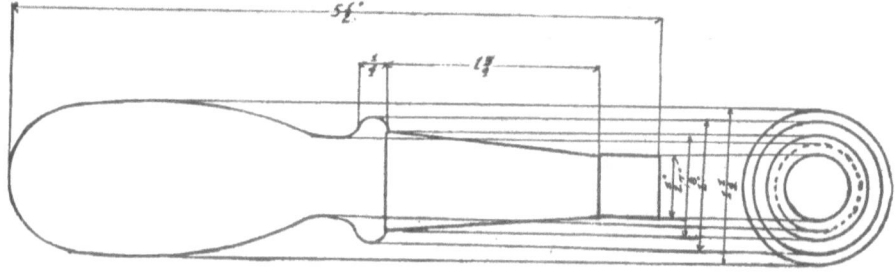

Model No. 18. - Paper Rack

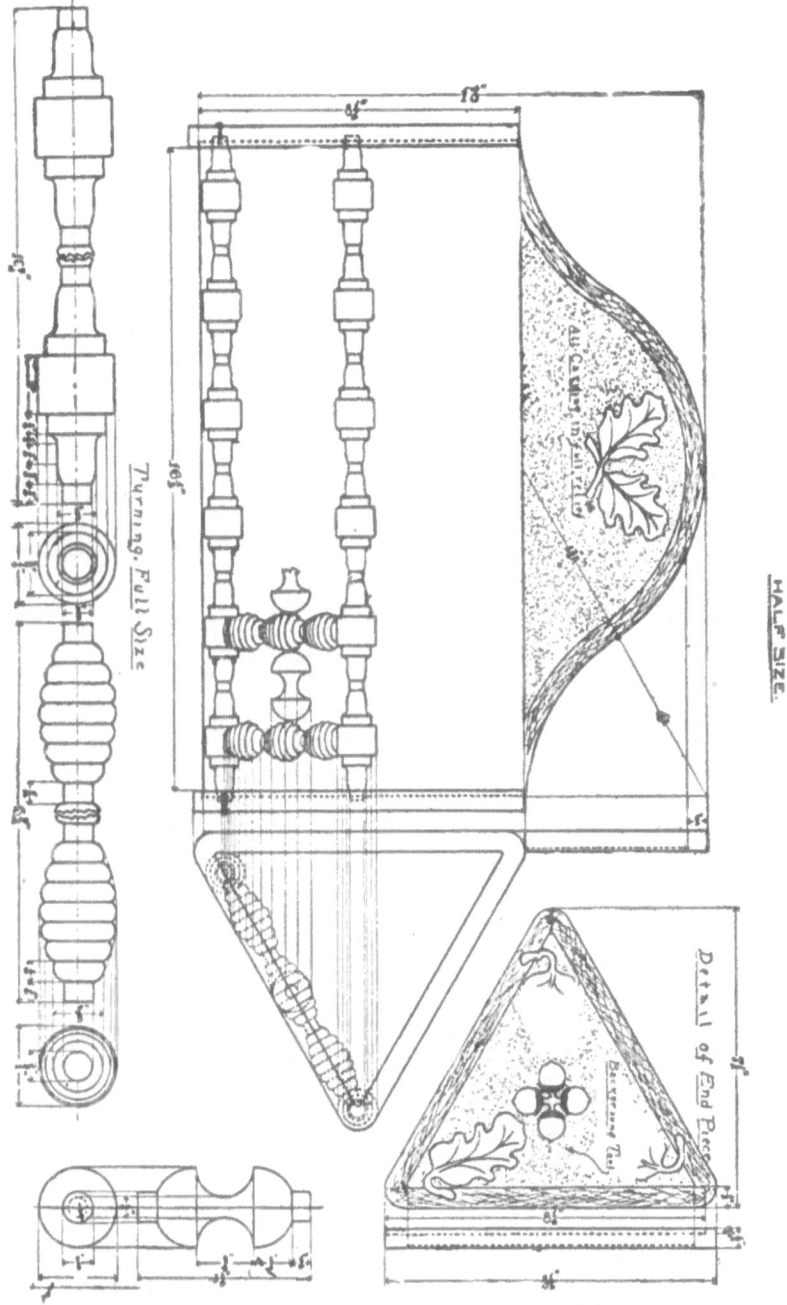

New Exercise: - Beading.   Tool: - 1-4 Chisel.
Tools for carving: - Same as in No. 15.

Model No. 19. - Bread Board

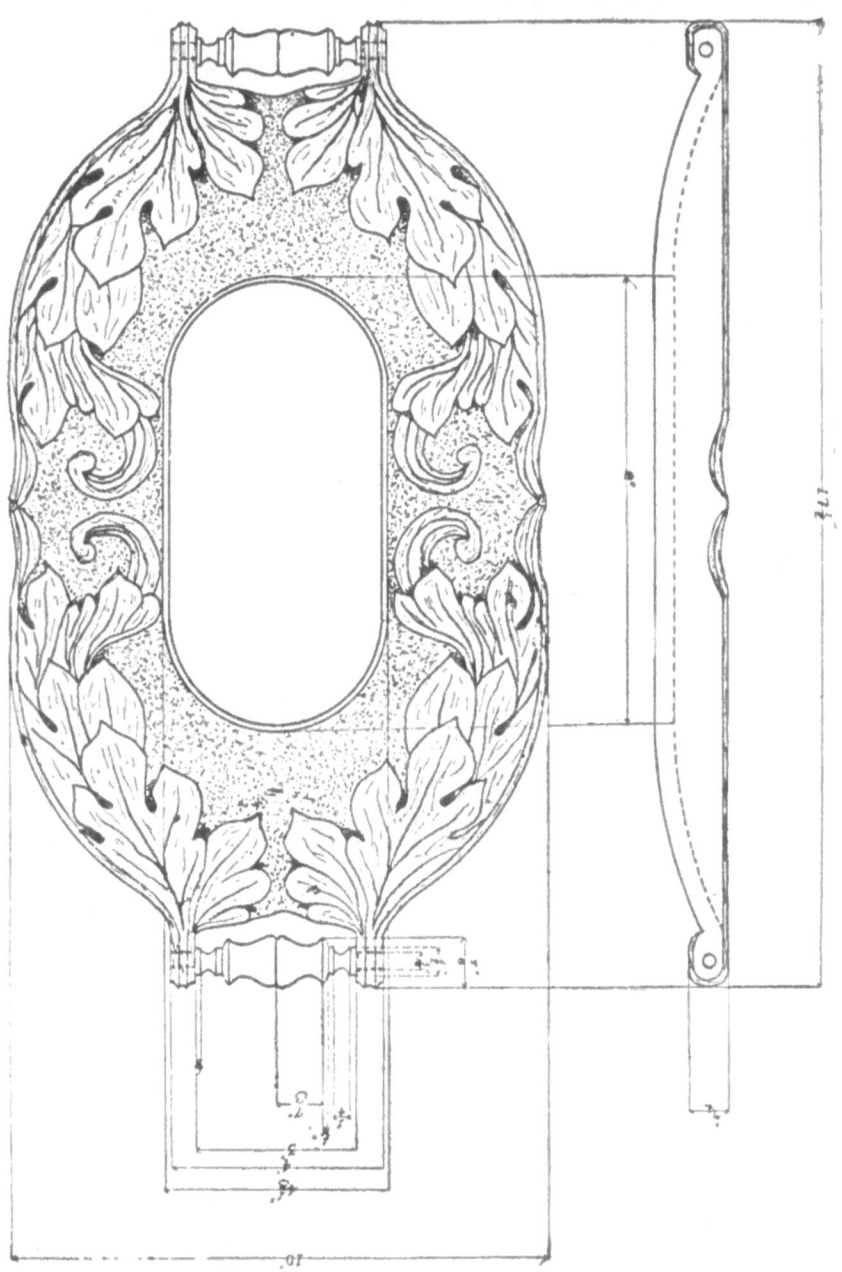

New Exercise in Carving: - Hollowing.
  Tool: - 1-4" flat gouge, 1-8" gouge, and same as in No. 15. Wood: - Gum wood.

Model No. 20. - Bill File

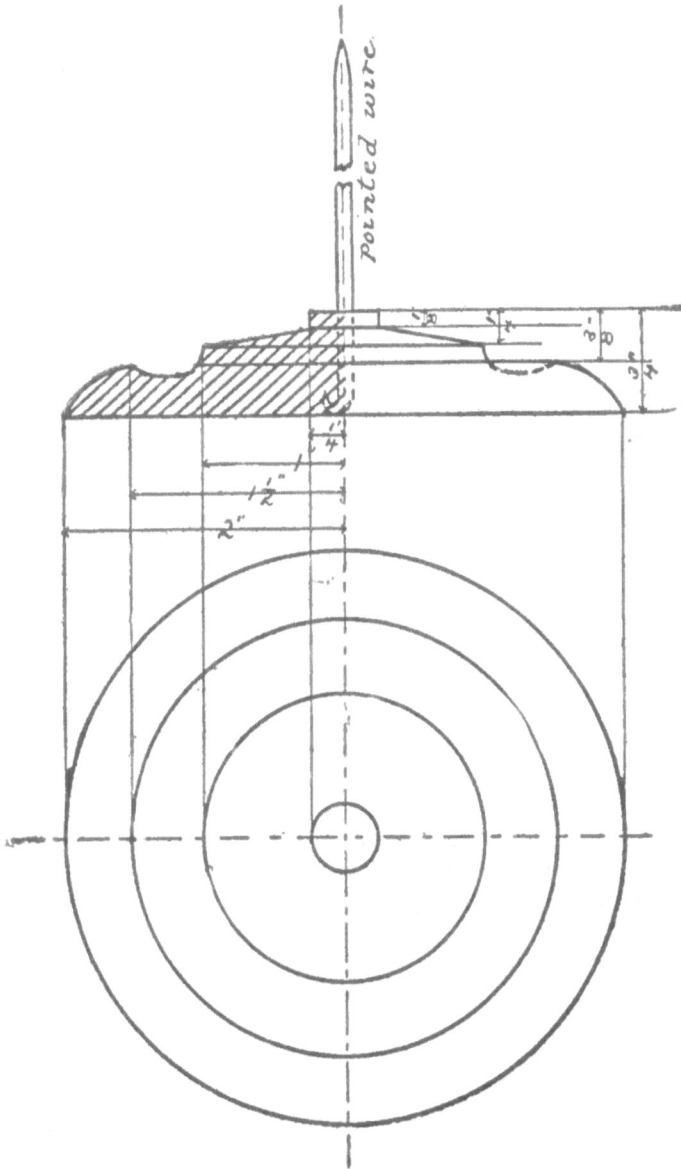

New Exercise: - Chuck-Turning.
   Tool: - Chisel and round-nosed tool. *Wood:* - Gum wood, oiled and shellaced.

Model No. 21. - Pulley Block

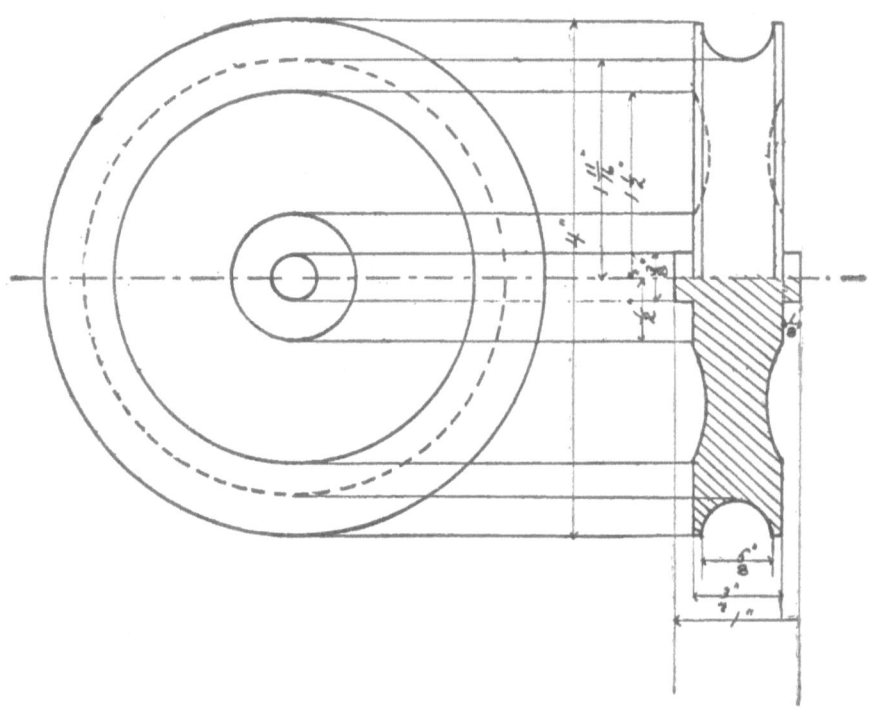

New Exercise: - Making and fitting box-chuck to turning.
Tools: - Round-nosed tool, gouge and chisel.
Wood: - Whitewood, oiled and shellaced.

Model No. 22. – Blotter

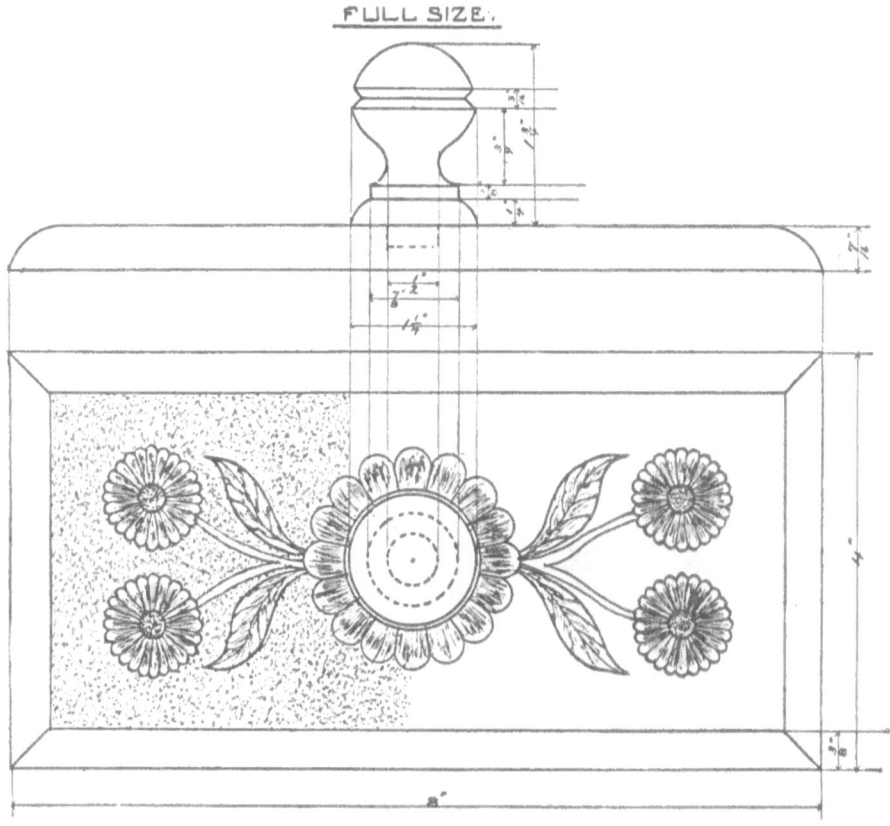

No New Exercise
Wood: - Gum wood, oiled and shellaced.

Model No. 23. - Paper Knife

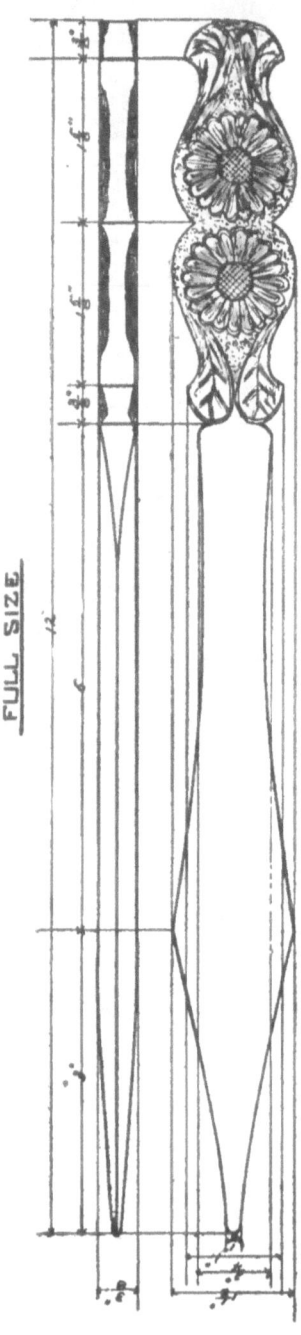

FULL SIZE

New Exercise: - Planing down, turning.
Wood: - Gum wood.

Model No. 24. Pen Holder

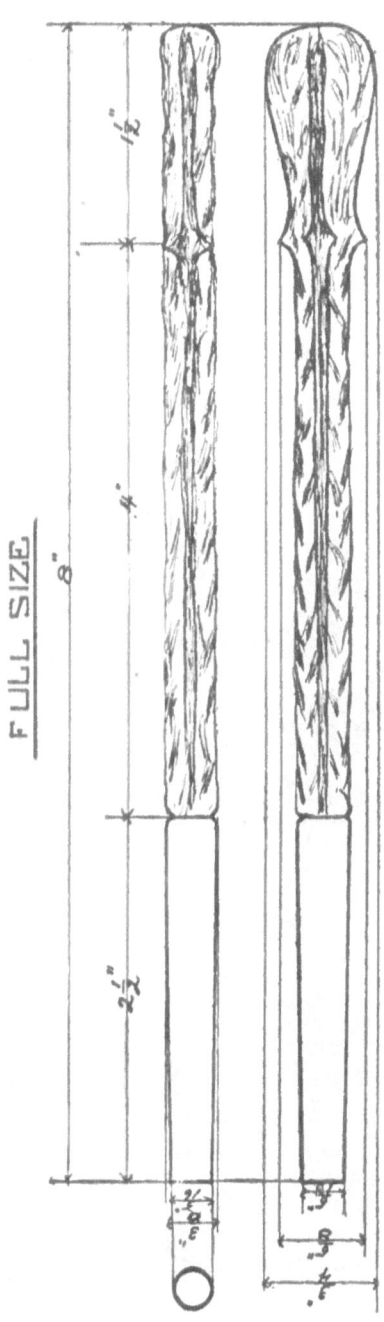

New Exercise: - Carring Cylinder.
Wood: - Gum wood, oiled and shellaced.

Model No. 25. - Ink Stand

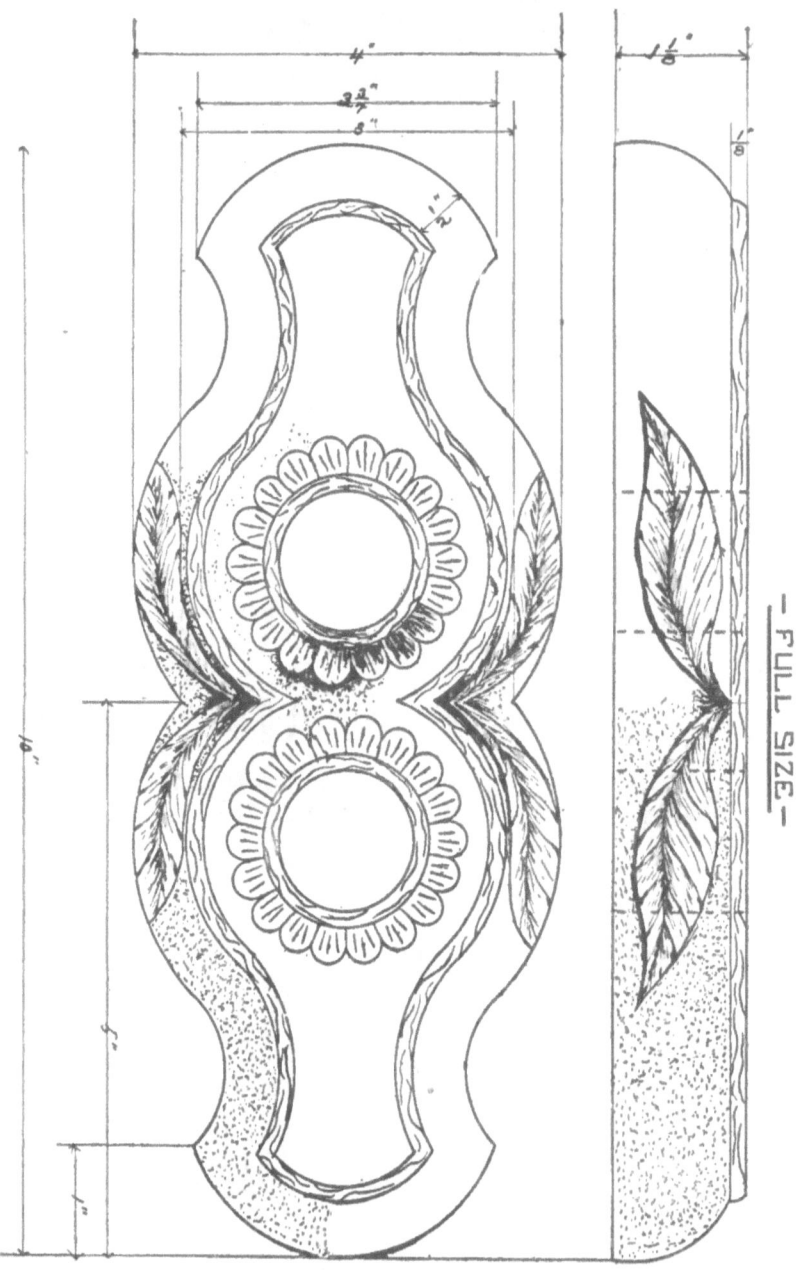

No New Exercise.
Wood: - Gum wood, oiled and shellaced.

Model No. 26. – Easel

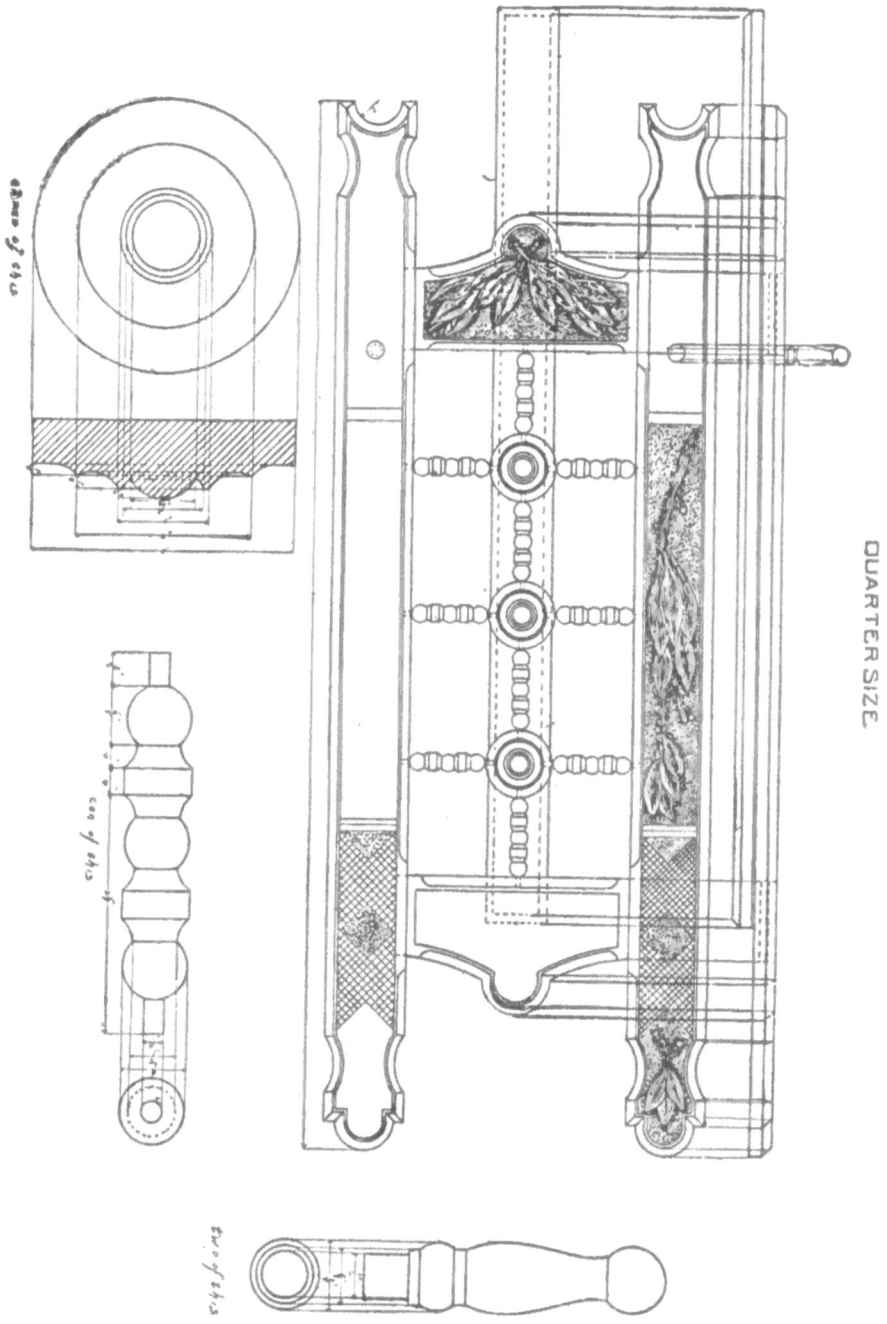

QUARTER SIZE

Test Model. Wood: - Gum wood, oiled and shellaced.

Model No. 27. - Powder Box

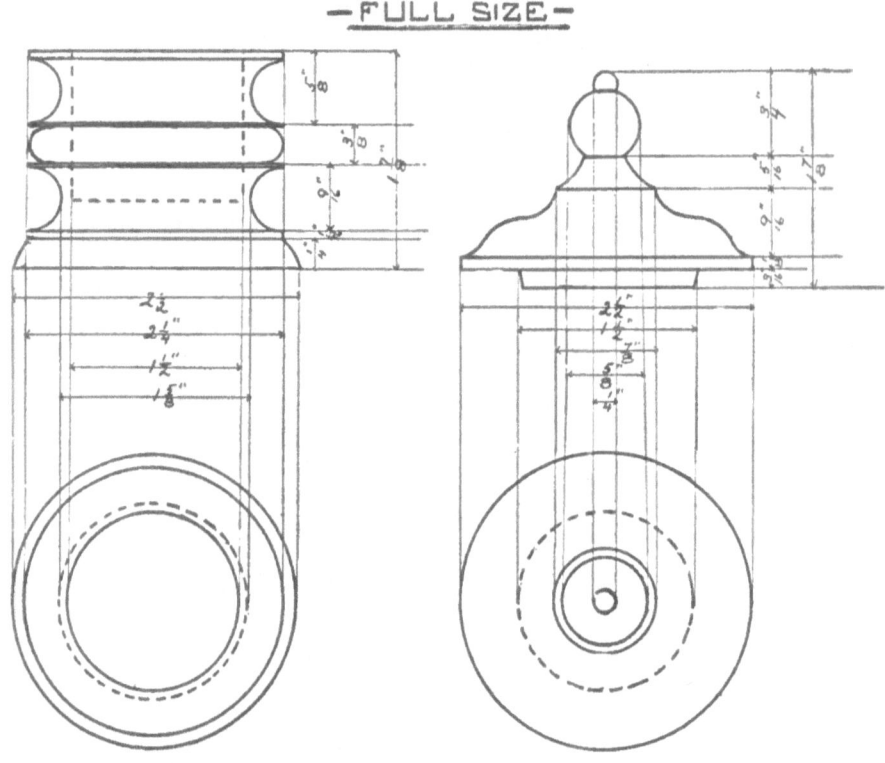

New Exercise: - Fitting
Wood: - Black walnut, oiled and shellaced.

Model No. 28. - Napkin Ring

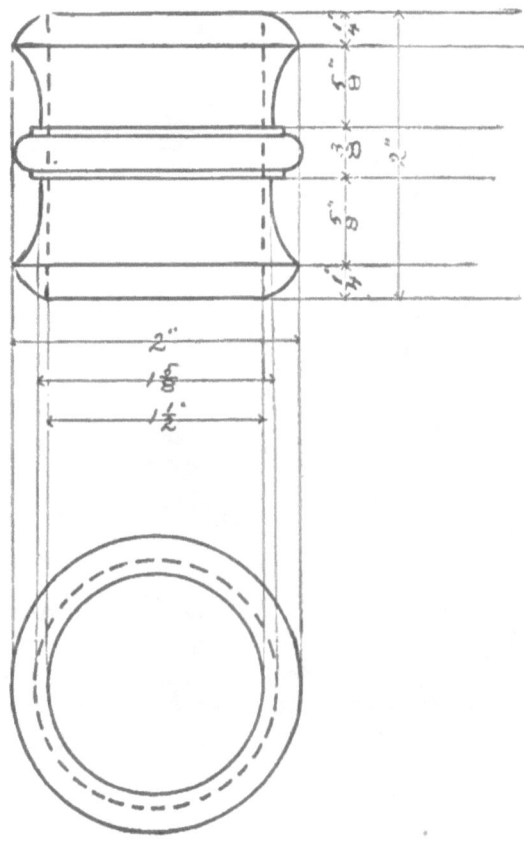

New Exercise: - Boring and fitting to cylinder for turning.
Wood: - Different kinds glued together, oiled and shellaced.

Model No. 29. - Butter Stamp

No New Exercise. Wood: - Whitewood.

135

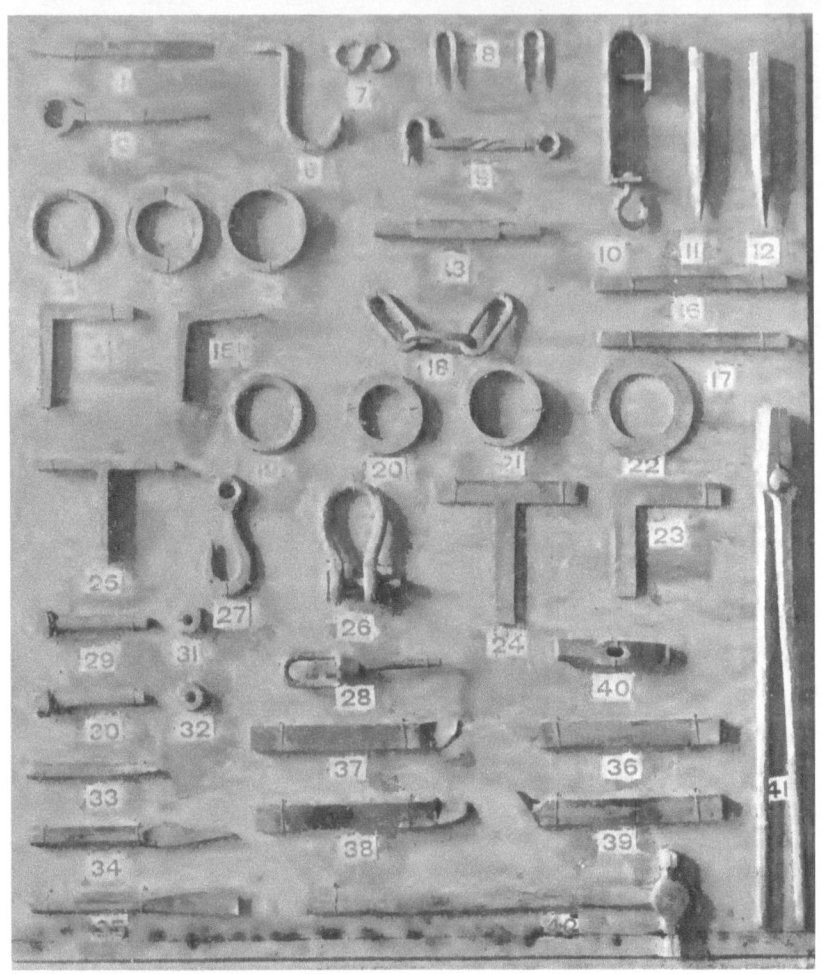

Series Six - Forging

The work in forging naturally follows the working in wood. It may also, be coexistant with it in the shape of pattern making, which should be preceded by instruction in moulding. The work with the forge is much different from anything that has gone before, except clay modelling. No better place is afforded the pupil for testing his eye, sense of form, his judgment of dimension, quantity, skill of hand, etc.

It is hard and often discouraging work but at the same time fascinating and highly educating. Here a change is made in regard to drawing. In the previous work the pupils have worked from their own drawings made from the study of the model; but now they are to make models from the study of prepared drawings.

Model No. 1. - Hammer Exercise

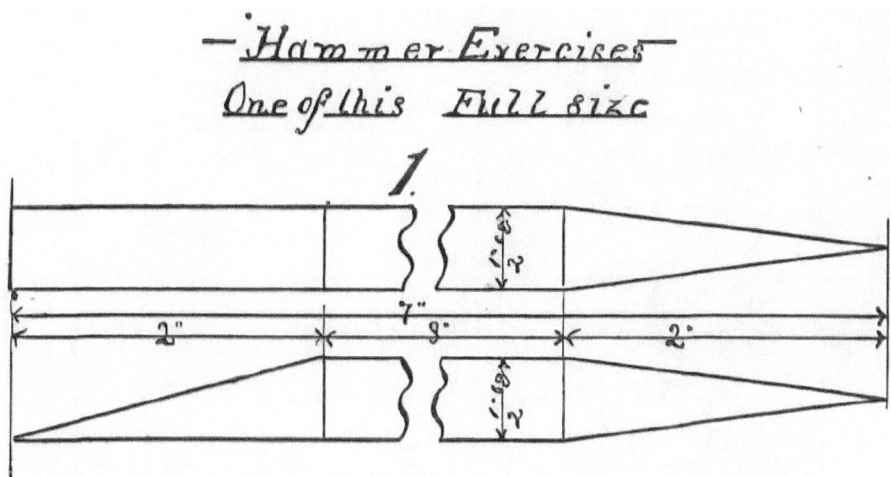

Take 5" of 3-4" round iron. Heat and draw down to 1-2" sq., tapering and pointing ends as shown in drawing, making wedge end first. Care should be taken not to burn iron in making pointed end.

Model No. 2. - Bending Exercise

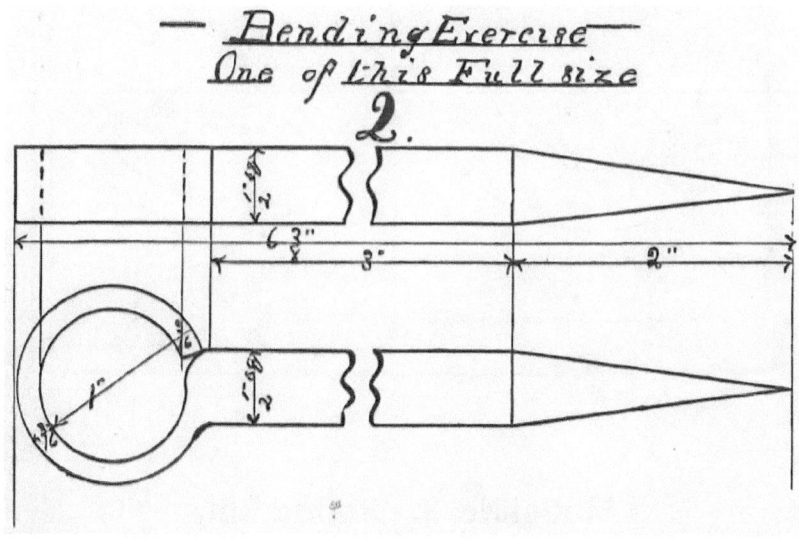

Take 5" of 1-2" sq. iron. Mark off from one end 1 3-4" with prick punch. Heat shoulder over round corner and draw out to 3-16" x 1-2" x 3 1-8". Heat and bend eye over horn. Heat and point the other end.

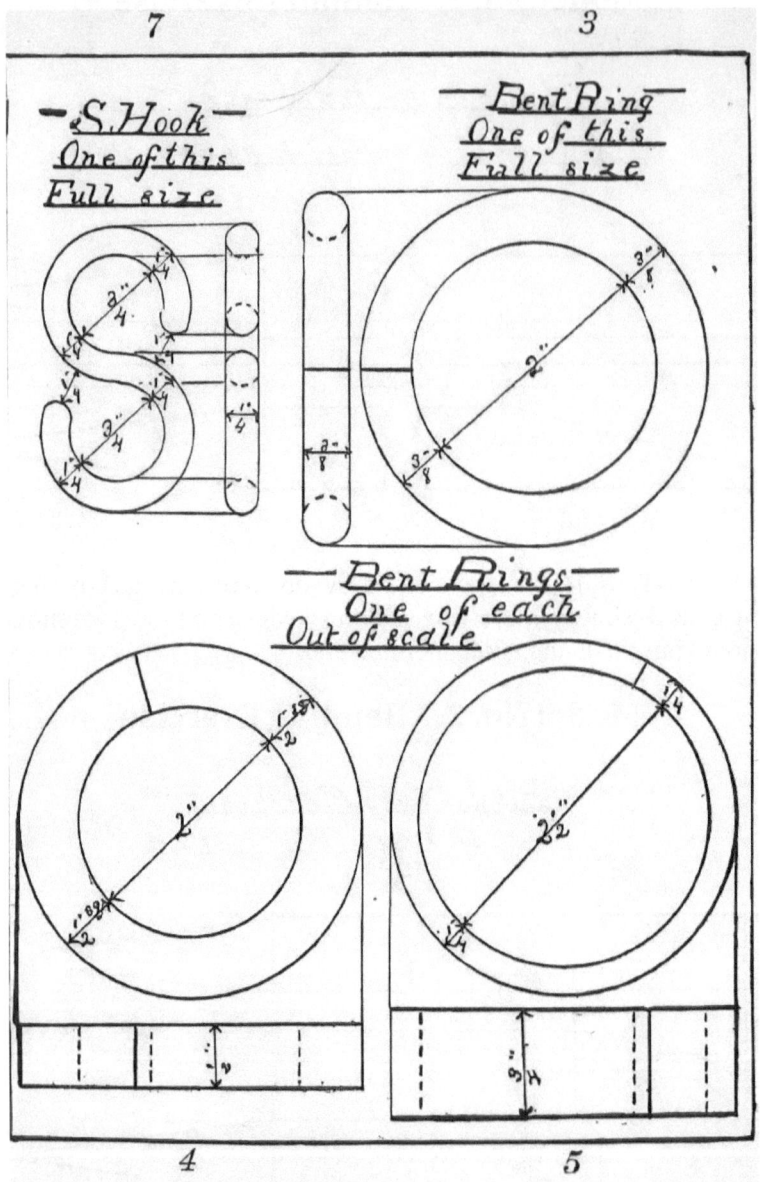

Model No. 3. - Round Ring

Exercise: - Bending.

Take 7 1-4" of 3-8" round iron. Heat and tap up ends, allowing for inside circle. Heat and bend to right size.

Model No. 4. - Square Ring

Exercise: - Bending.

Take 7 3-4" of 1-2" sq. iron and proceed as in No. 3.

Model No. 5. - Flat Ring

Exercise: - Bending.

Take 9" of 3-4" x 1-4 iron and proceed as in No. 3.

Model No. 7. - S Hook

Exercise: - Bending.

Take 5" of 1-4" round iron. Round ends and bend according to drawing.

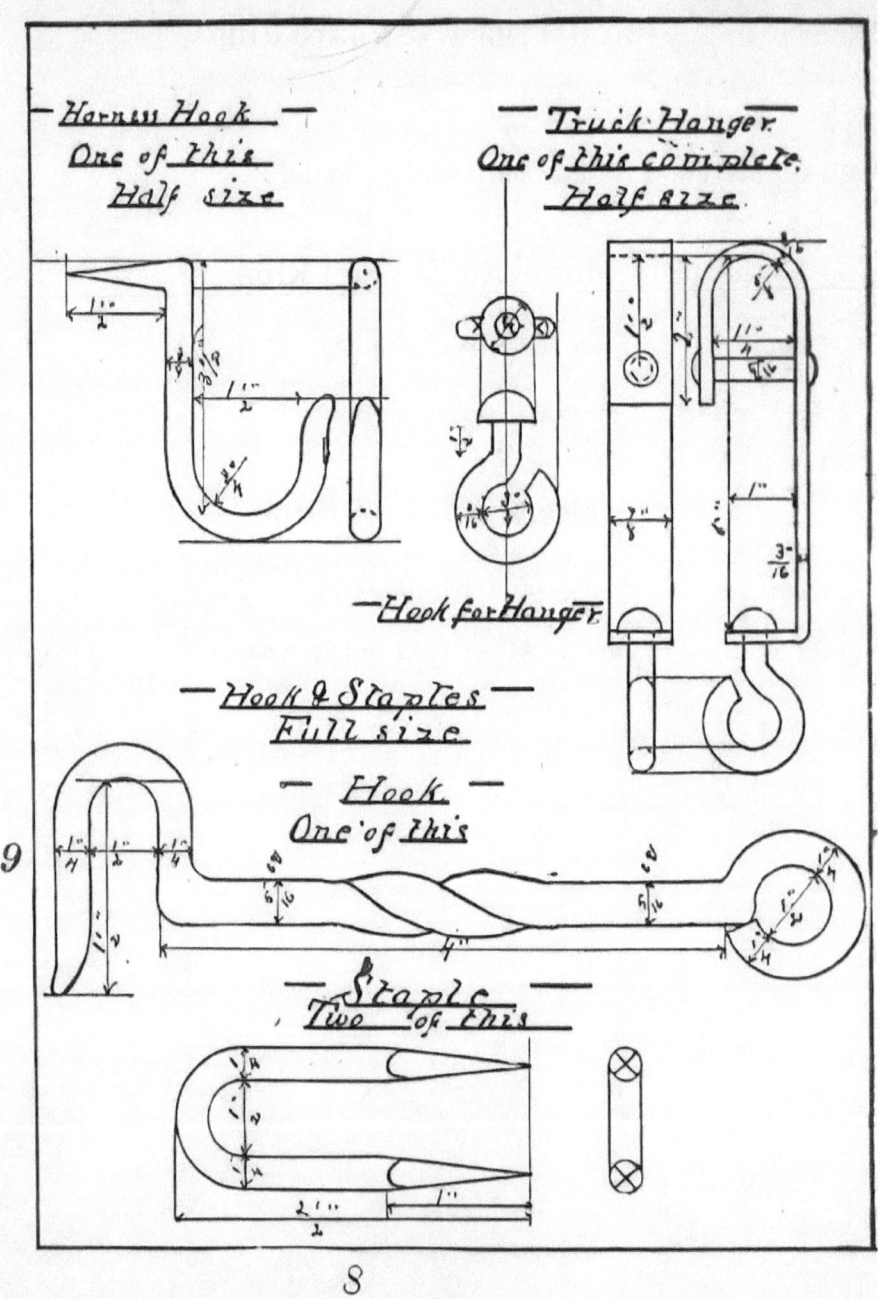

Harness Hook —
One of this
Half size

— Truck Hanger.
One of this complete.
Half size.

—Hook for Hanger

— Hook & Staples —
Full size

— Hook. —
One of this

9

—Staple.—
Two of this

Model No. 6. - Harness Hook

Exercise: - Bending and shouldering.

Take 7 1-4" of 3-8" round iron. Point and bend according to drawing, bending hook first.

Model No. 8. - Staples

Exercise: - Pointing and bending.

Take 3 5-8" of 1-4" round iron. Point and bond according to drawing. Special care should be taken not to burn ends.

Model No. 9. - Hook

Exercise: - Bending, Pointing and Twisting.

Take 8" of 5-16" round iron. Draw down 2" for eye and bend. Mark oft* from shoulder of eye 4 1-8"; draw out on other end 2 1-2" for hook, point and bend hook according to drawing, heat body grasp with two pairs of tongs and twist 180°

Model No. 10. - Truck Hanger

Exercise: - Punching, Riveting and Heading.

Take 9 1-4" of 7-8" x 3-16 iron. Square ends; punch hole 3-8" from end and bend shoulder; punch holes 3 1-2 and 7 1-2 from shoulder, bend and rivet together, using vice in riveting. Next take 3 1-2" of 5-16" round iron for hanger, upset one end and head in heading tool, bend hook using bolt tongs in bending.

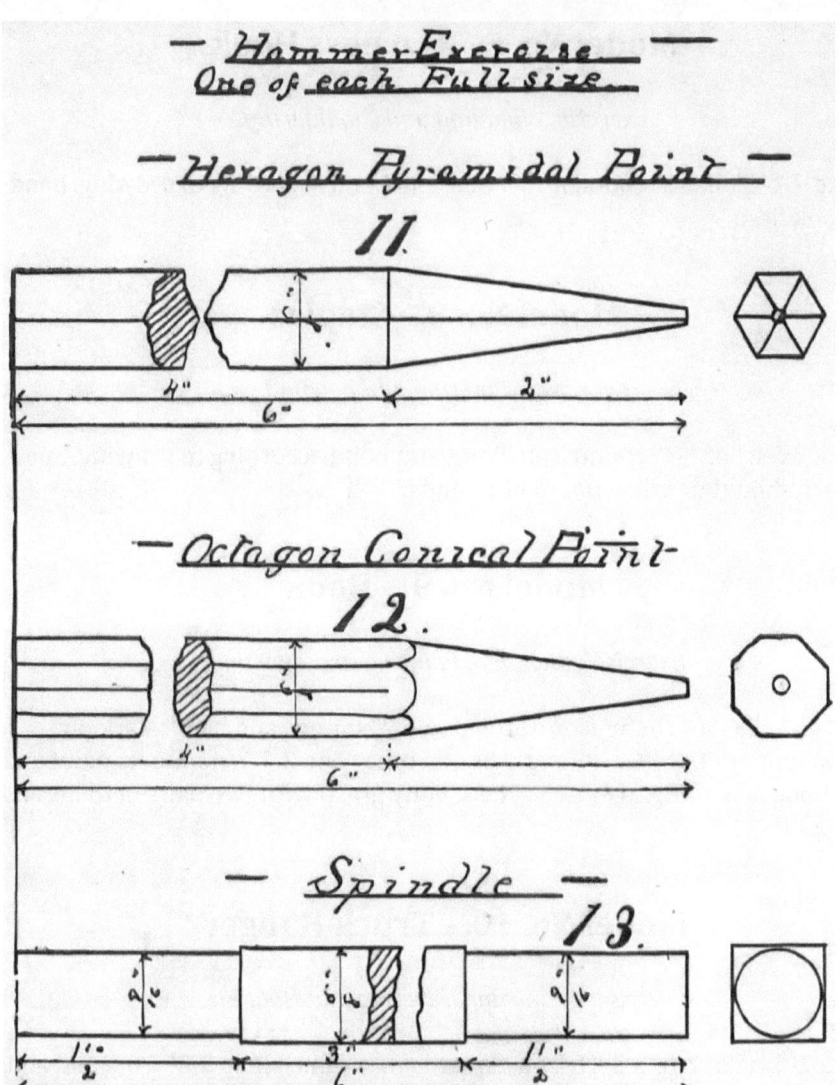

Model No. 11. - Hexagon with Pyramidal Points

Take 5" of 3-4" round iron; hammer to hexagon; draw out one end to pyramidal point.

Model No. 12. - Octagon with Conical Point

Take 5" of 3-4" round iron; hammer to 5-8" octagon; draw out one end to conical point.

Model No. 13. - Spindle

Exercise: - Swaging.

Take 6" of 5-8" square iron, hammer ends to 9-16" round; draw out ends to 9-16" round, using swage for finishing.

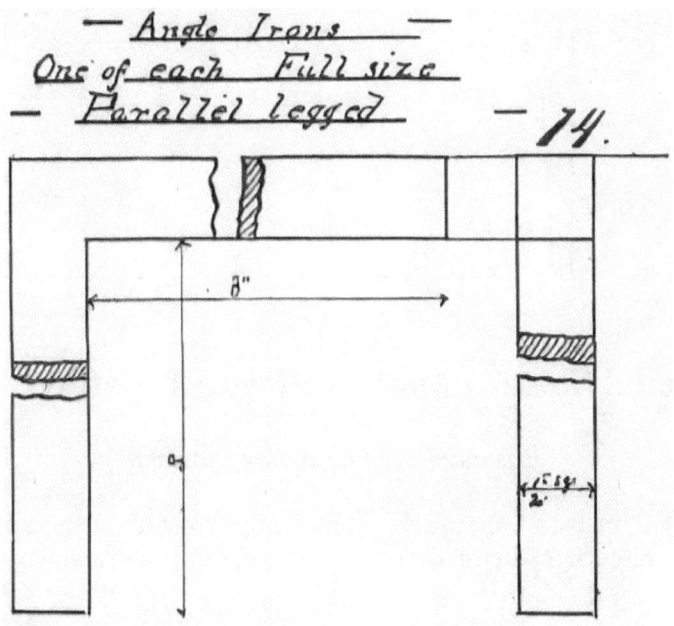

Model No. 14. - Angle Iron, Parallel Legs

Exercise: - Making Square Corners.

Take 8" of 1-2" square iron; upset as in No. 14 and bend over square corner of anvil, finish according to drawing.

In welding, special care should be taken to keep the fire clean in order to insure a good weld, and high, to prevent the blast from cooling the iron.

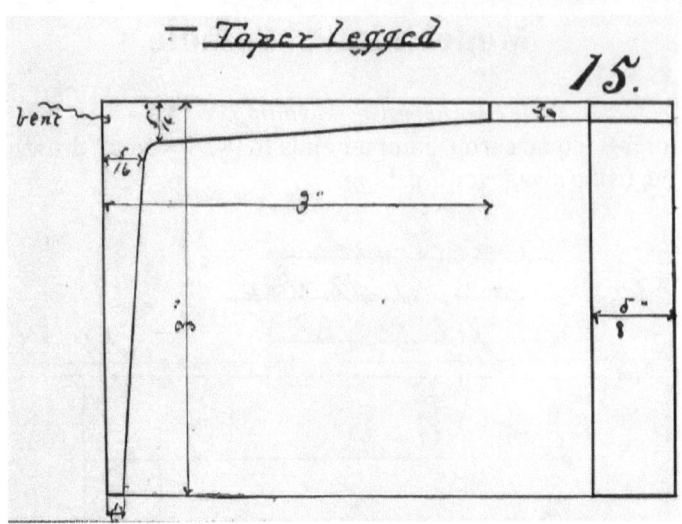

Model No. 15. - Angle Iron with Tapered Legs

Exercise: - Bending Square Shoulder.

Take 4 1-2" of 1-2 x 5-8", upset in center, bend over round corner of anvil, making outer corner square; draw out legs according to drawing.

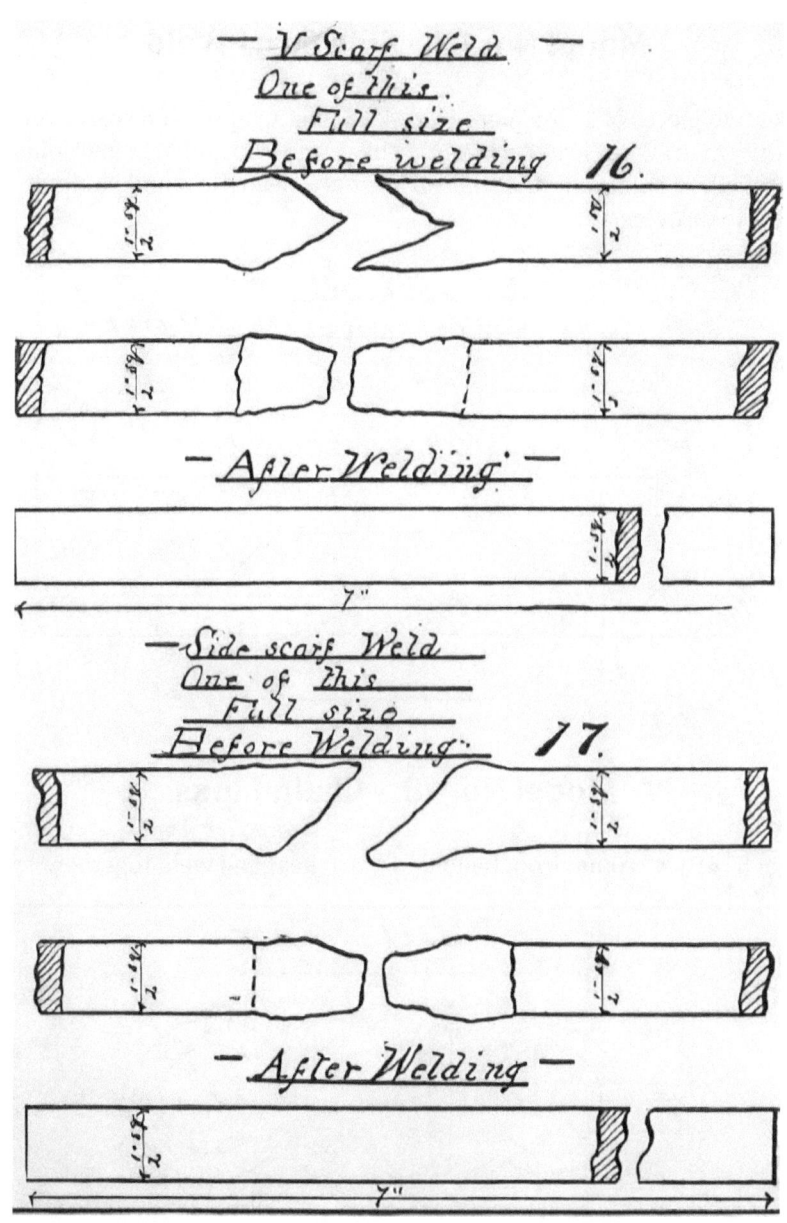

V Scarf Weld
One of this.
Full size
Before welding 16.

After Welding.

7"

Side scarf Weld
One of This
Full size
Before Welding. 17.

After Welding

7"

Model No. 16. - V Scarf Weld

Take two pieces of 1-2" square, 4" in length; upset and scarf as shown in drawing, making V with cold chisel; place the pieces together before heating and proceed as in No. 16.

Model No. 17. - Side Scarf Weld

Take two pieces of 1-2" square iron, 4" in length; upset and scarf over anvil as shown in drawing, heat to a welding heat, and with aid of helper join and weld together, being sure that the surfaces are clean. Heat and hammer according to drawing.

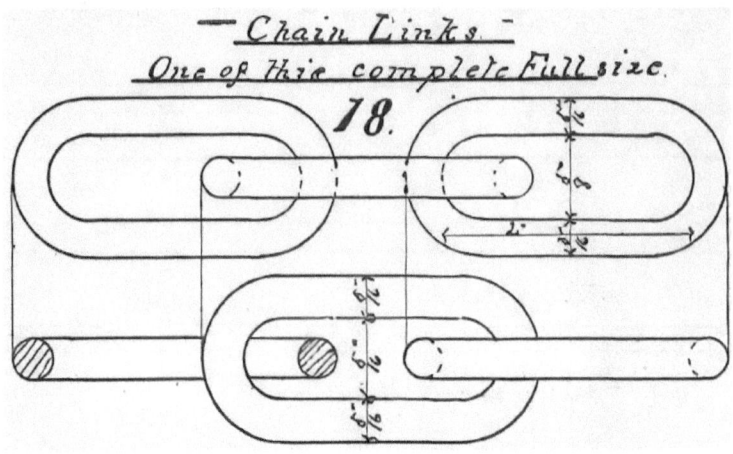

Model No. 18. - Chain Links

Take 5" of 1-4" round iron; bend and scarf; heat and weld together.

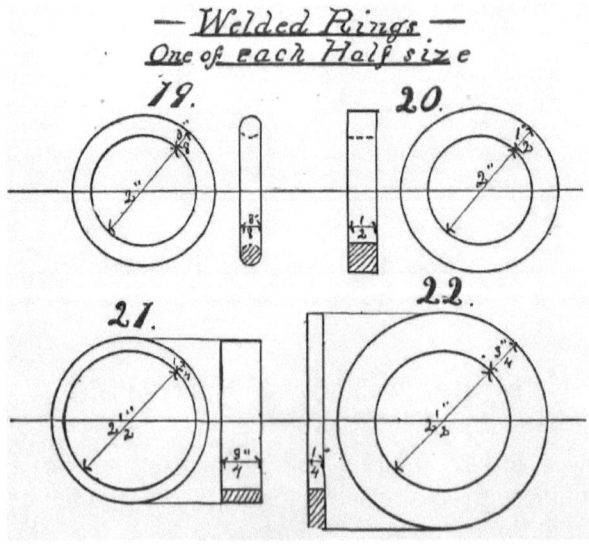

Model No. 19. - Welded Rings

Take 8" of 3-8" round iron; upset and side scarf, weld together.

Model No. 20. - Square Rings

Take 7 3-4" of 1-2" square iron; upset scarf, and proceed as with previous models.

Model No. 21. - Flat Rings

Take 9" of 3-4" x 1-4" iron; upset, scarf, and proceed as with previous models.

Model No. 22

Take 10 3-8" of 3-4" x 1-4" iron; upset, scarf, and weld together.
Note. The first three rings are welded over horn; the last is welded on face of anvil.

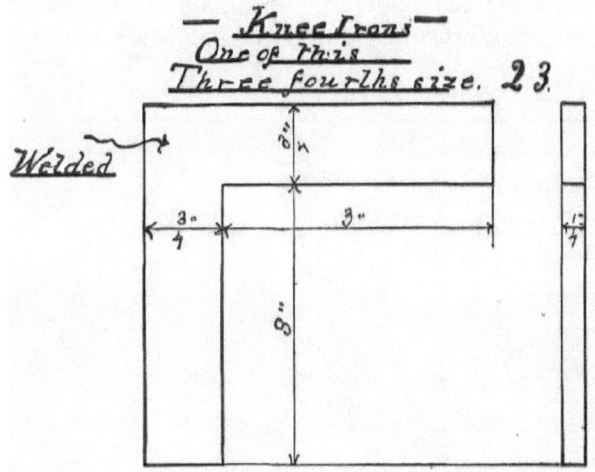

Model No. 23. - Knee Iron

Take two pieces of 5 3-4" of 3-4" x 1-4" iron: upset, scarf, and weld with aid of helper.

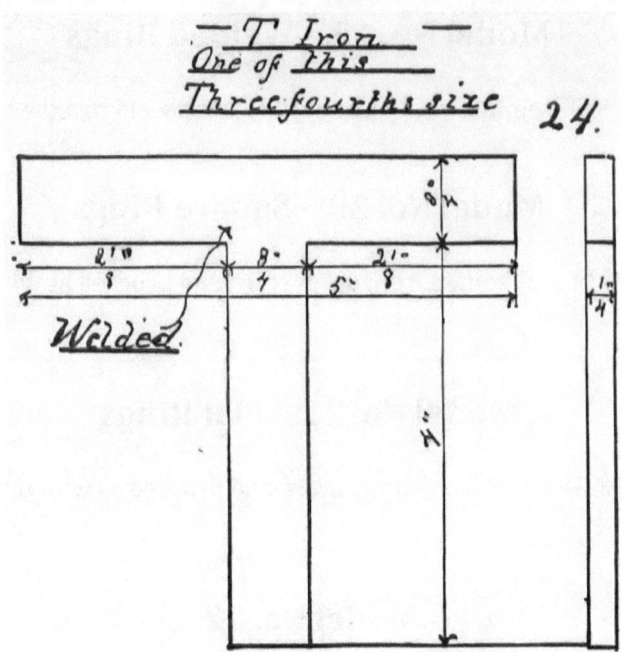

Model No. 24. - T Iron

Take one piece 6 1-2" and another 5 3-4" of 3-4" x 1-4"; scarf and weld.

Note. The different scarfs in welding should be made in lead by the teacher before the class.

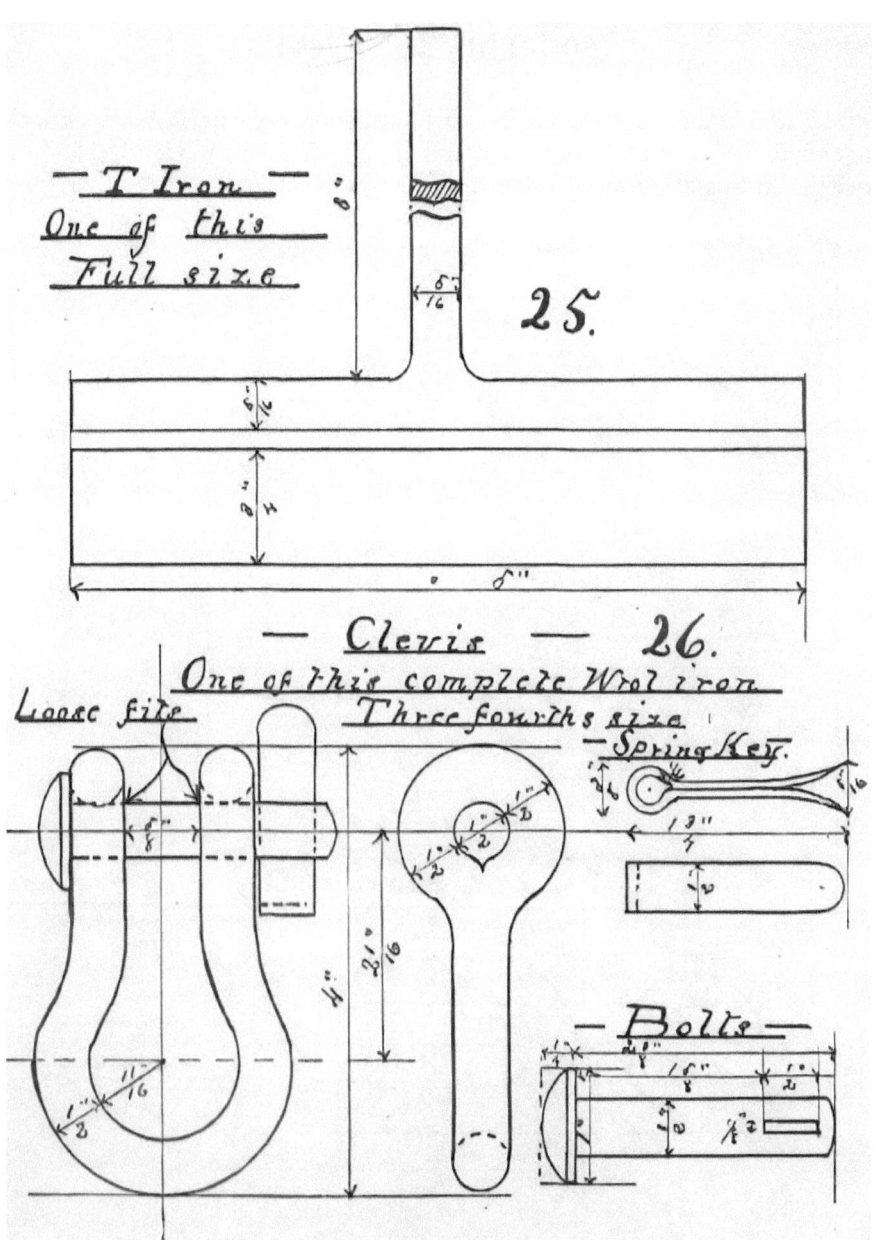

- T Iron -
One of this
Full size

25.

— Clevis — 26.
One of this complete Wrot iron
Three fourths size

Loose fite

— Spring Key.

— Bolts —

Model No. 25. - T Iron

Take one piece 6 3-4" and another one 5" of 3-4" x 5-16" iron. Take the 5" piece; upset, split with aid of cold chisel, drawing ends out and at right angle to body. Upset other piece in middle; make hollow for scarf. Weld together with aid of helper.

Model No. 26. - Clevis

Take 14 1-2" of 1-2" round iron; scarf both ends; bend and weld eyes according to drawing. Make bolt, heat and punch eye for spring key. Make spring, bending eye around 1-4" iron.

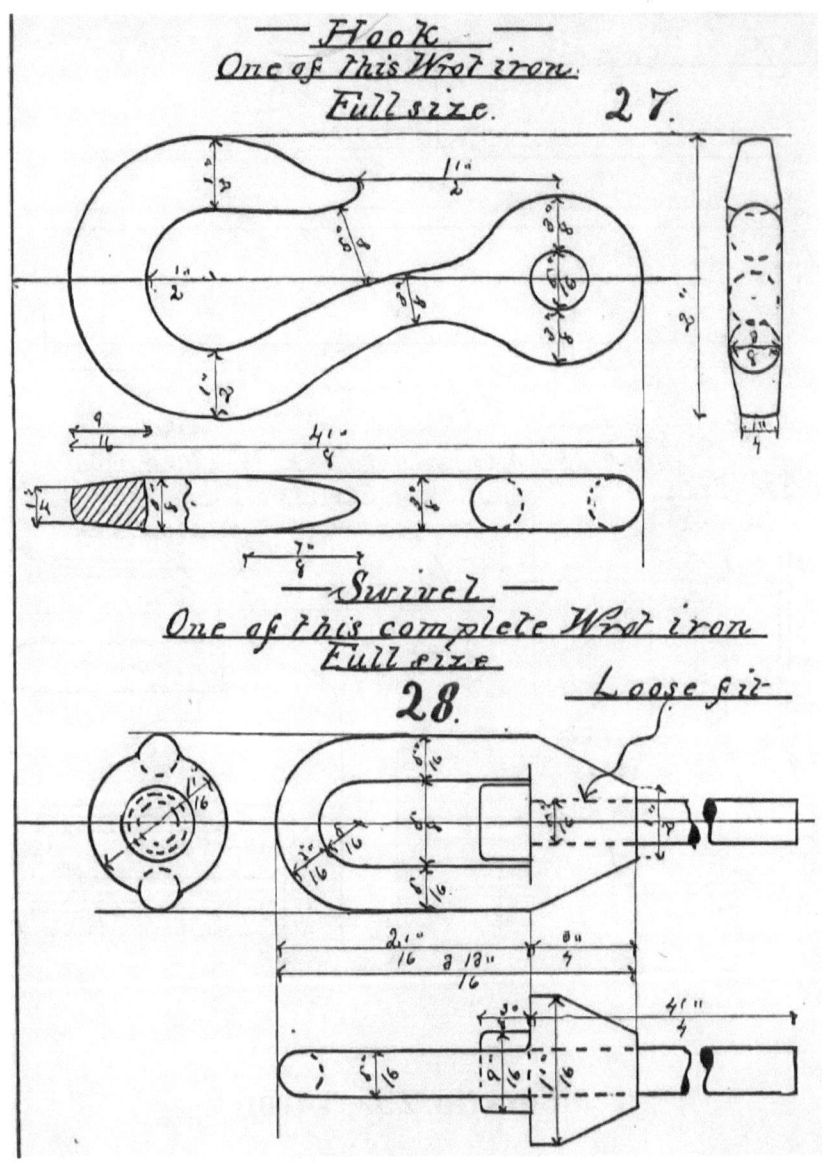

Model No. 27. - Hook

Take 7 3-4" of 1-2" round iron; upset end, flatten and punch eve and finish over horn. Point other end and bend according to drawing.

Model No. 28. - Swivel

Take 5 1-4" of 5-16" round iron; scarf and bend. Take 7-8" of 7-8" x 1-2" iron; punch hole and shape for body; weld this to the prepared piece; take 4 5-8" of 5-16" round iron for bolt; for head of bolt take a piece long enough to go around bolt: bend this round the end of bolt; heat and weld together.

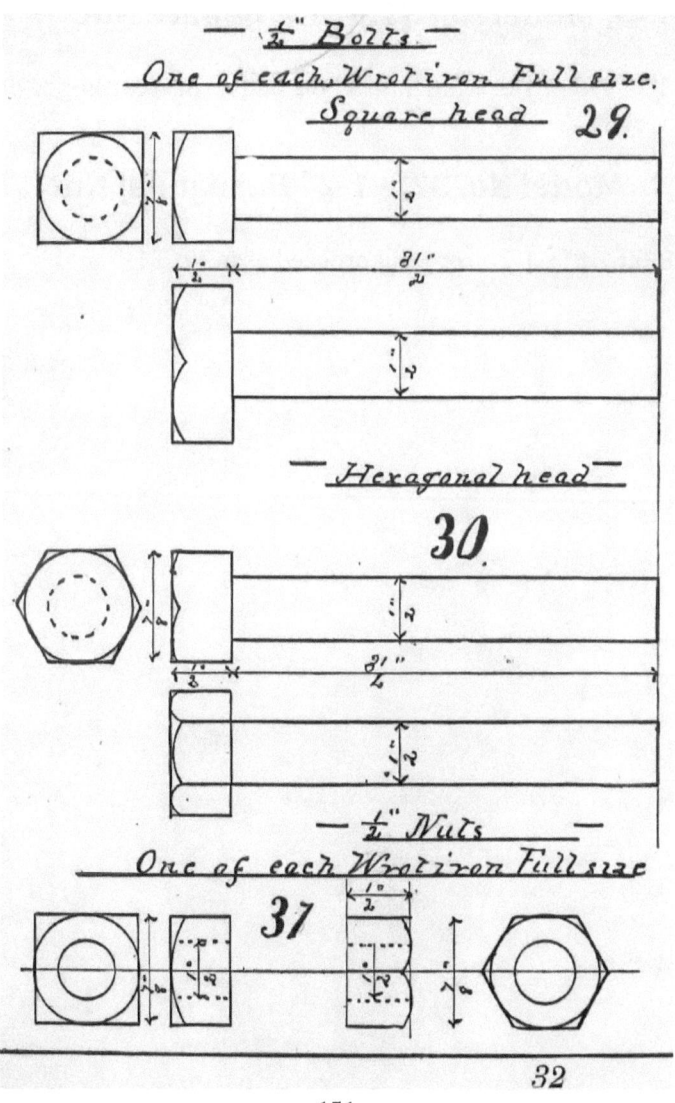

Model No. 29. 1-2" Suare Headed Bolt

Take 4" of 7-8" x 3-4" iron; draw down with aid of swage and head with aid of heading tool.

Model No. 30. - 1-2" Hexagonal Headed Bolt

Proceed with the making as in No. 29.

Model No. 31. - 1-2" Square Nut

Take 7-8" of 7-8" x 1-2" iron; punch hole and form according to drawing.

Model No. 32. - 1-2" Hexagonal Nut

Take 7-8" of 7-8" x 1-2" iron; and proceed as in No. 31.

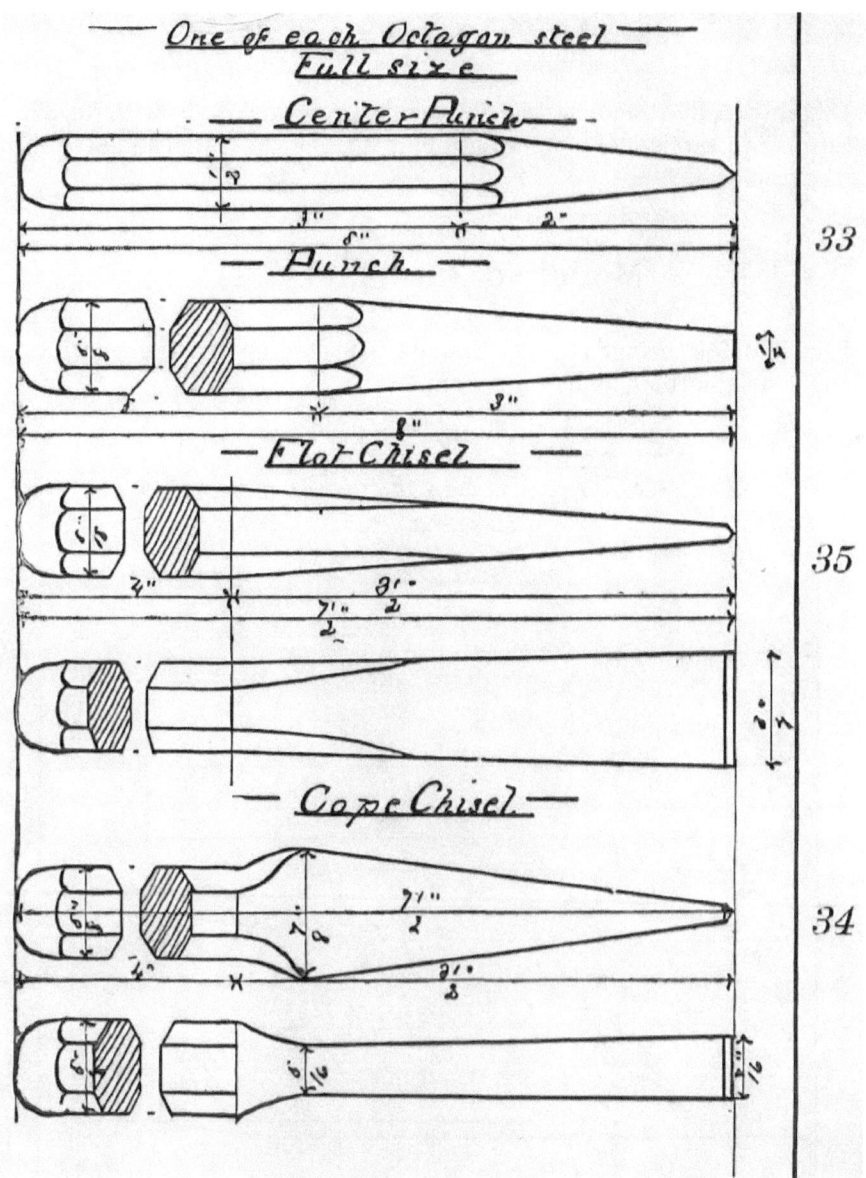

Model No. 33. - Octagonal Center Punch

Take 4 1-2" of 1-2" octagonal steel, bevel, handle according to drawing, draw out point according to drawing and temper.

Note. Care should be taken not to burn steel, for burned steel is worthless.

Model No. 34. - Cape Chisel

Take 1" of 5-8" octagonal steel. Proceed with the making as with No. 32.

Note. The exercises of tempering should be fully illustrated and explained by the teacher.

Model No. 35. - Flat Chisel

Take 7" of 5-8" octagonal steel. Round end according to drawing; draw out, cutting end according to drawing; temper.

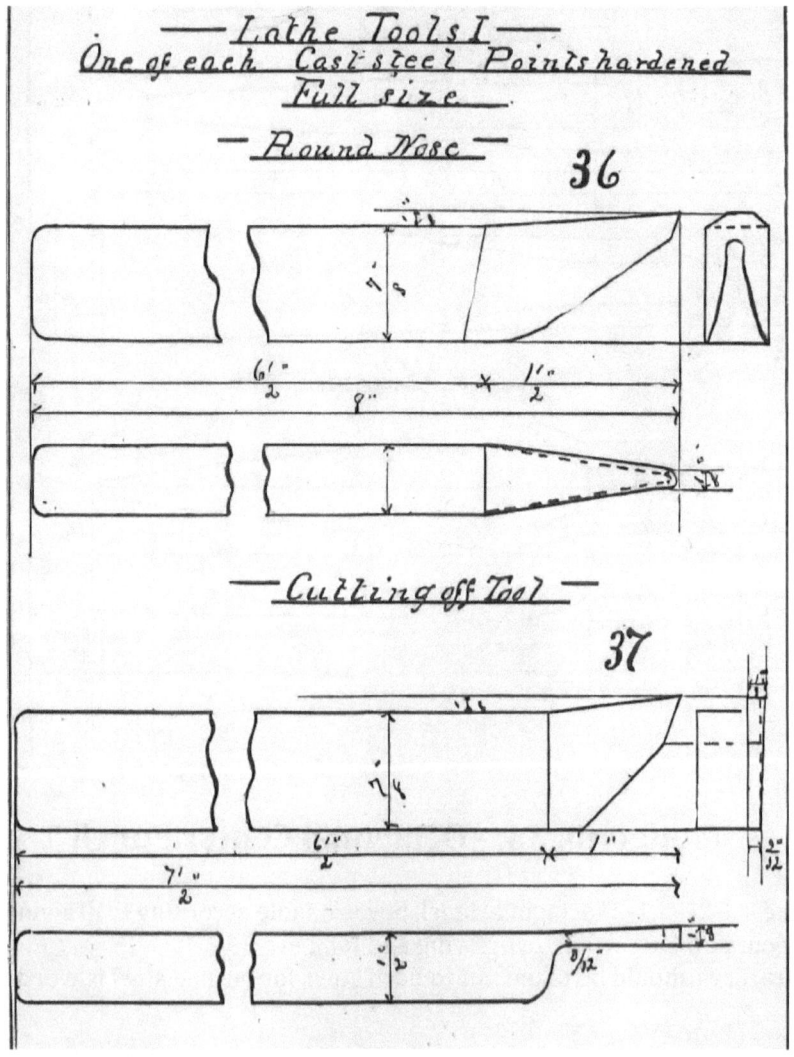

Model No. 36. - Round-Nosed Lathe Tool

Take 7 3-4" of 7-8" x 1-2" steel. Round end and draw out point according to drawing; temper.

Model No. 37. - Cutting-Off Tool

Take 7" of 7-8" x 1-2" steel. Round end; form cutting-end according to drawing.

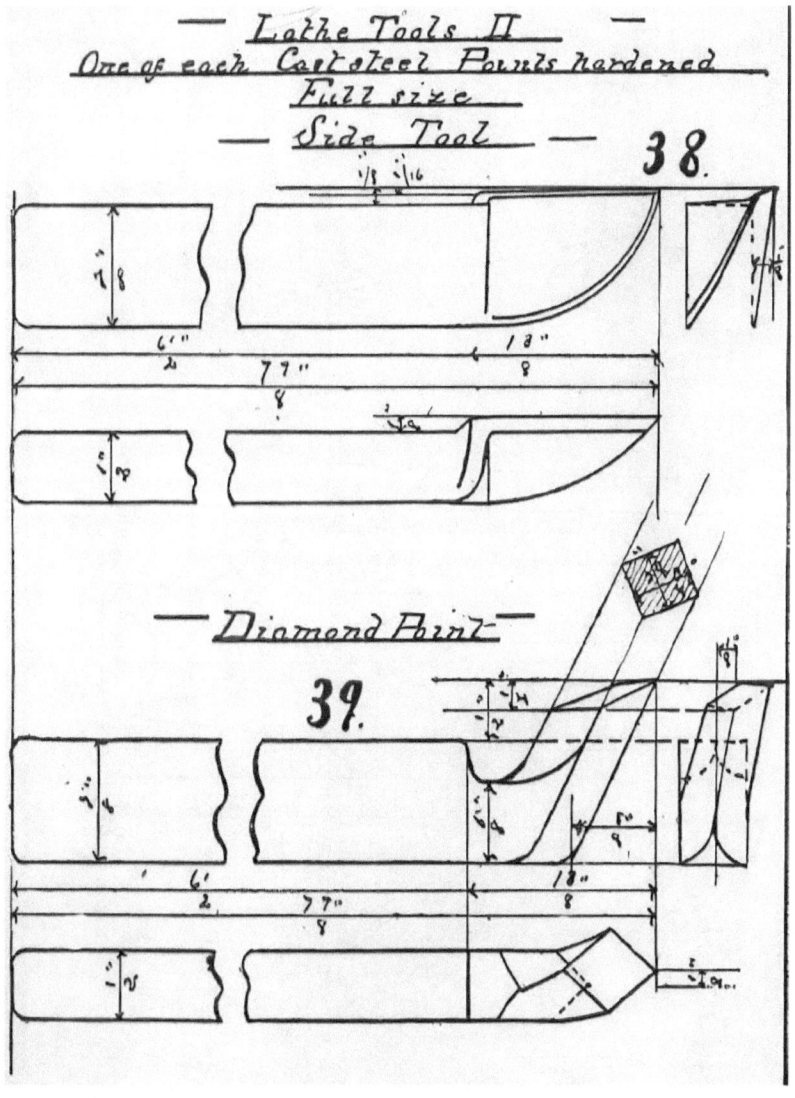

Model No. 38. - Side Tool

Take 7 3-4" of 7-8" x 1-2" steel; round end, and point according to drawing; temper.

Model No. 39. - Diamond Point

Take 7 1-2" of 7-8" x 1-2" steel; round end; draw out and point.
Note. The last model should be worked in lead before attempting it in steel.

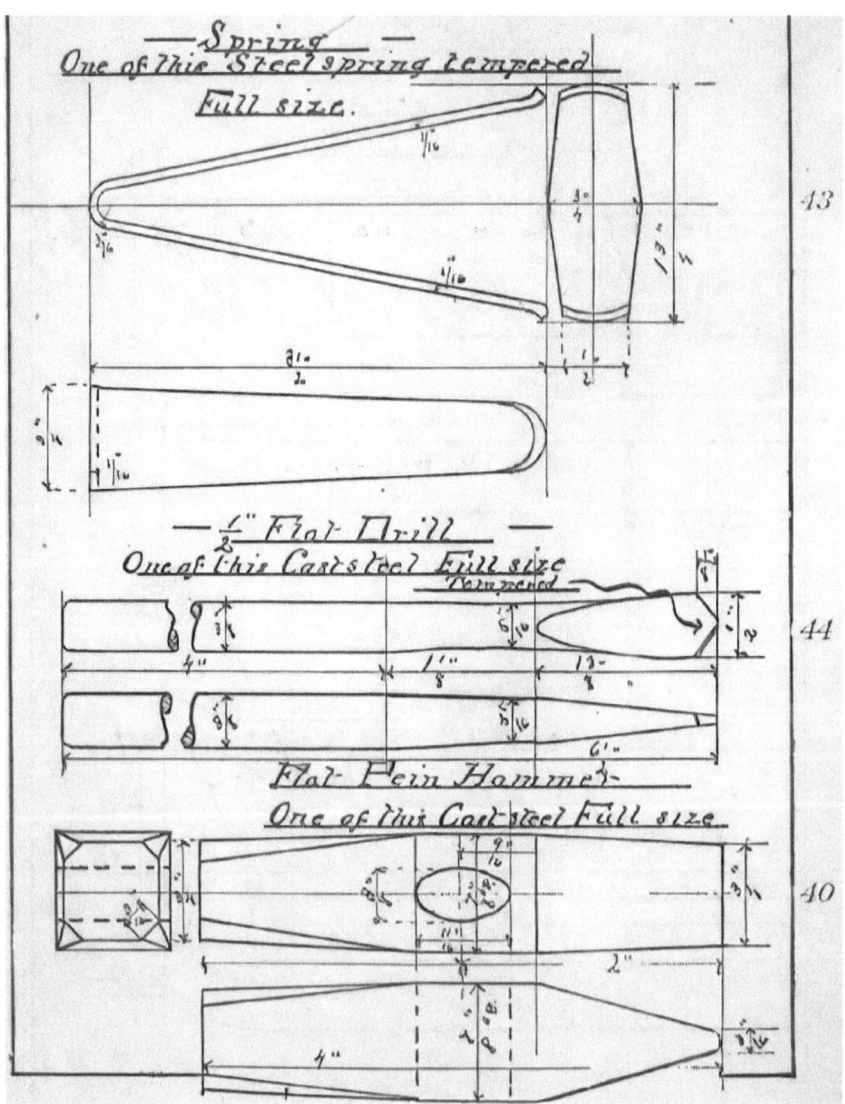

Model No. 40. Flat Pein Hammer

Take 3 3-4" of 7-8" square steel; punch eye and draw out according to drawing.

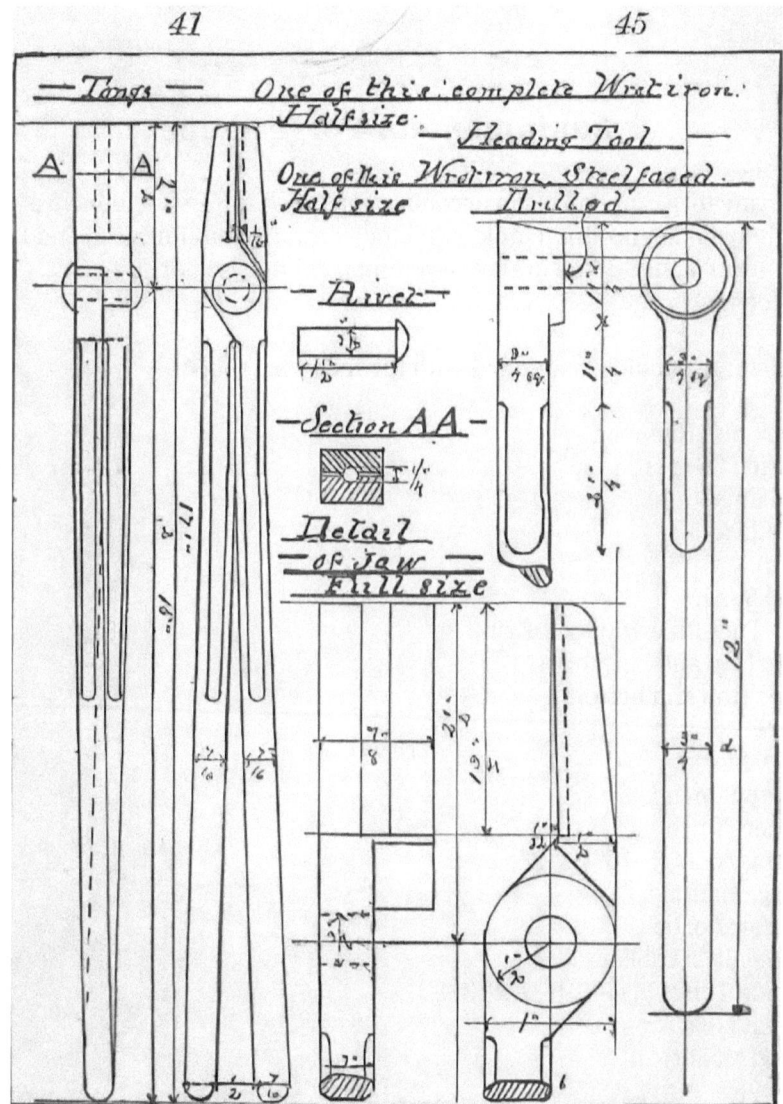

Model No. 41. - Tongs

Take 6" of 1" square iron; form jaw on both ends of piece and punch holes; cut in center; draw down; form and weld handles to these. Make and place rivet.

Model No. 42. - Machinist Hammer

Take 3 3-4" of 1" x 1" steel; upset in center; punch eye and shape with aid of fuller; draw out ends, finishing with swage and file.

Equipment for Forge Shop

As many forges as room can accommodate, each forge should have a poker, shovel, sprinkler, hod, and tank with blower attachment for blast, and fan for carrying off smoke, if the draft of a common chimney is not sufficient. One anvil for each forge.

Each forge should be supplied with the following tools:

1 Machinist Hammer
1 Outside Caliper
1 Cold Chisel
1 Hot Chisel
1 Hardy
1 Steel Square
1 Two-Foot Rule with brass rim.
Fullers (top and bottom).
Swages (top and bottom).
1 Flatter
Copper Blocks
1 Round Punch
1 Center Punch
Heading Tools (5-16" x 1-2")
1 Sledge Hammer
1 Leather Apron
1 Course Bastard File
Common Tongs (1-4" 3-8" 1-2" 3-4")
Bolt and Link Tongs
1 Wood Mallet
1 Iron Vice

www.ingramcontent.com/pod-product-compliance
Lightning Source LLC
Chambersburg PA
CBHW051832170626
46807CB00003B/1144